MW01026031

"I've never been more concerned about the moral and spiritual condition of our nation, and I know millions of Americans feel the same. In *Toward a More Perfect Union*, my friend and colleague Tim Goeglein articulates his own grave concerns, offering a frank assessment of our present educational system and its neglectful treatment of U.S. history and civics. Tim's insights are eye-opening, and his prescription for addressing this problem offers hope for a brighter future here in America."

—Jim Daly, president, Focus on the Family

"The United States is in the midst of widespread political unrest, social incivility, and cultural deterioration to an extent virtually unknown in our history. In his latest book, *Toward a More Perfect Union: The Moral and Cultural Case for Teaching the Great American Story*, author Tim Goeglein has provided an astute and fascinating examination of this perilous situation and also discusses the actions an aroused citizenry must adopt to renew a solid foundation for our constitutional republic. Based upon his incisive analysis of our national condition and its moral and intellectual underpinnings, this is an important book that will interest and benefit every concerned reader."

—Edwin Meese III, Ronald Reagan distinguished fellow emeritus, the Heritage Foundation; and former U.S. attorney general

"Not content with the national loss of historical memory and the accompanying loss of the American dream, Tim Goeglein offers a vision of a way forward, a recovery of zeal for this nation, the 'last, best hope of mankind.'"

—Alan E. Sears, founder, Alliance Defending Freedom

"The American story is the most noble, inspiring lesson in all of human history—which Tim Goeglein captures eloquently in *Toward a More Perfect Union*. Most importantly, Tim offers hope for rejuvenating our collective belief in a bright American future, by reclaiming our understanding of American history."

—Kevin D. Roberts, PhD, president, the Heritage Foundation; and American historian

"In *Toward a Perfect Union*, Tim Goeglein expertly dissects one of the main issues facing our country today: the lack of civic education and the distortion of American history that presently holds sway throughout all levels of our nation's educational system. The result is tragic, as we see whole generations who have little or no idea of how the government works or of the sacrifices made to create the freest nation on earth. Tim provides an adroit and cogent prescription for what ails our country: the renewed commitment to teaching the great American story, so future generations will once again appreciate their God-given liberty while regaining respect for our country and each other."

—The Honorable Kay Coles James, Virginia
secretary of the commonwealth

"Tim Goeglein loves America, and his insightful book makes the case for protecting America's future by authentically teaching its past. The accurate teaching of history and civics is foundational to good education and good citizenship, and *Toward a More Perfect Union* paves the way for a much-needed renewal of the way we teach the story of America."

—Shawn D. Akers, online provost, Liberty University

"Memory is a crucial resource for a sound future. Just as it is a tragedy when memory is lost for an individual, it is tragic when a civilization loses its own story. America cannot survive without its history told and remembered correctly. In *Toward a More Perfect Union*, Tim Goeglein makes a powerful case for recovering civic education and the accurate telling of American history, citing allies on both the political Right and the Left to do so. This book is a gift."

—John Stonestreet, president, the Colson
Center; and host, *BreakPoint* podcast

"Our education system is in shambles—and it is producing a citizenry who not only misunderstands its past but misunderstands itself as a consequence. Tim Goeglein's *Toward a More Perfect Union* is precisely the bracing antidote necessary to counteract the poison being pumped into our children—poison that will bear hideous fruit if it is not combatted."

—Benjamin Shapiro, editor emeritus, *The Daily Wire*; and host, *The Ben Shapiro Show*

"*Toward a More Perfect Union: The Moral and Cultural Case for Teaching the Great American Story* is a well-thought-out defense of American patriotism as a means for our nation to avoid the mistakes of the past. Rather than simply identifying the current problem of historical ignorance, Tim lays out the blueprint for how each citizen of the United States ought to learn, preserve, and retell the true story of our country, both the good and the bad—and thus work toward a society made up of selfless individuals who seek unity in caring for the well-being of all persons, particularly the most vulnerable."

—Marjorie Dannenfelser, president, Susan B. Anthony Pro-Life America

"Poll after poll, as well as anecdotal evidence, shows that Americans are increasingly ignorant of our nation's founding story and how our institutions are meant to work for the common good. This has resulted in great division instead of common unity. In *Toward a More Perfect Union*, Tim Goeglein examines how we got to this point and the steps we can take to come together as Americans. I highly recommend it."

—Penny Nance, president, Concerned Women for America

"In his thoughtful and scholarly examination of America's culture and the teaching of American history, Tim Goeglein seeks to 'point a way forward out of the morass of partisan historical bickering toward a truly unified and truly conservative vision of our nation.' He exposes the '1619 Project' as an attempt to 'radically rewrite American history' and falsely depict America as a state 'motivated and sustained by racism.' Tim's vision—and mine—is to unite the American people around 'a deep, honest exploration of our shared past—the good and the bad.' This timely book provides a path and the tools to attain that vital objective."

—Star Parker, founder and president,
Center for Urban Renewal and Education (CURE)

"For decades, American students have either received little to no education about our history and government, or if they have received an education, it has been a distorted view that seriously misrepresents the intentions and motives of our Founding Fathers. In *Toward a More Perfect Union*, Tim Goeglein refutes this misinformation while providing a framework for teaching our children about their God-given heritage of freedom and how it can be preserved for future generations."

—David Barton, founder, WallBuilders;
and Tim Barton, president, WallBuilders

# TOWARD A MORE
# PERFECT
# UNION

Timothy S. Goeglein

# TOWARD A MORE
# PERFECT
# UNION

## The Moral and Cultural Case
## for Teaching the Great American Story

FIDELIS
PUBLISHING

FIDELIS PUBLISHING®

ISBN: 9781956454130
ISBN (eBook): 9781956454147

*Toward a More Perfect Union*
*The Moral and Cultural Case for Teaching the Great American Story*
© 2022 Tim Goeglein

Cover Design by Diana Lawrence
Interior Design and Copyedit by Lisa Parnell

Order at www.faithfultext.com for a significant discount. Contact info@fidelispublishing.com for discounts on bulk purchases.

Fidelis Publishing, LLC Sterling, VA • Nashville, TN fidelispublishing .com

Manufactured in the United States of America

10 9 8 7 6 5 4 3 2

FOR JENNY, TIM, PAUL, BEVERLY, AND STANLEY.
*You are the loves of my life, and you continue to show me that the best life is the one enveloped in unconditional love, given and received. Soli Deo Gloria!*

# *Contents*

# Introduction

*If we forget what we did, we won't know who we are.
I'm warning of an eradication of the American memory that
could result, ultimately in an erosion of the American spirit.*[1]

RONALD REAGAN

*Over the course of an entire generation,
educational professionals have reduced history to nearly
an elective. This decision has produced a spike in
polarization, incivility, and general apathy. It is in the
national interest to revitalize our approach to teaching history:
the subject is part of the intellectual infrastructure
so important for the nation's long-term civic health.*[2]

HOWARD MUNCY

It was about ten years ago when I first met my good friend Craig.

While we both worked in conservative politics and non-profit organizations for nearly thirty years and saw each other from a distance at various events, our paths never crossed until we were introduced by a mutual friend, Alan Sears.

*1*

Once we met, we quickly realized we were intellectual soulmates. Both of us have a passion for history, a love of country, and concern for future generations. We both grieve the devastation to America's culture wrought by radical activists who are indoctrinating our nation's youth. We both bemoan the lack of a firm but reasoned response from those who love our nation and its history, while those who react in anger rule our national discourse.

We agree all are created *imago Dei*—in the image of God—and as such, we are called to treat all others, even those with whom we strongly disagree, with dignity and respect.

Secondly, it has sadly become evident over the past seventy years, Americans have become increasingly ignorant of our nation's founding principles. Civic education and American history have either not been taught or have been deliberately mistaught throughout our nation's public—and in numerous cases, even our private—education system. This lack of education or misinformation has placed our nation in great peril, and we are seeing the consequences unfold daily in our corporate boardrooms, halls of power, and streets.

The result is the American crisis we are experiencing today.

Across our nation, there is a fundamental misunderstanding of how government works, what powers it rightly has, and how it can justly use those powers. Whole generations have grown up without understanding basic economics, mistrusting the motives of our nation's Founding Fathers, and spurning and vilifying those who have made immense sacrifices to create, and then preserve, our constitutional republic.

A huge number of our fellow Americans not only despise the foundational values of our culture; they even despise the idea of extending basic civility toward others, regardless their views. This ignorance and disdain plays itself out in all aspects of our culture—whether it be mob attacks on statues and monuments; younger generations' embrace of socialism; widespread disrespect of parents by both children and the government; disparagement of religion, law enforcement, and the military; or venomous rhetoric spewed at our fellow citizens as often seen in social media comments when people mock the beliefs, heritage, and ideas of others in the most disparaging terms. It is also demonstrated daily on CNN, MSNBC, Fox News, and other media outlets.

There is a direct tie between our civic and historical ignorance and how we treat each other as human beings. It is not a coincidence the coarsening of our national discourse began when we removed civics, religion, and history from our education system. Soon after, we began to teach distorted forms of each, and the sickness in our discourse metastasized.

Yes, our history is not perfect because flawed human beings made it, and there are aspects that should be taught—such as slavery, the "Trail of Tears," or the internment of peaceful Japanese Americans during World War II—so we do not make the same mistakes again, but these attacks have resulted in us losing a united purpose as a nation.

Craig and I came to these conclusions from our own unique perspectives. While we are only a few years apart in age, we grew up with vastly different experiences based on geography. I grew up in the Midwest—Indiana, to be exact—while Craig was raised an hour north of San Francisco in the beautiful wine country of Sonoma County. I received a traditional American history and civic education, but Craig experienced something completely different. He received a preview of coming attractions—i.e., the revisionist teaching of American history—firsthand before its poisonous roots spread across our entire land.

As I wrote earlier, we both love history. Craig recalls the time back in the mid-1960s when he and his family made their annual Christmas trip to downtown San Francisco to do shopping, ride the rooftop rides, and visit Santa Claus. This was still in the era of the great department stores when Christmas shopping was an event, not an ordeal. Going to "The City" meant dressing up and being on your best behavior.

A highlight was lunch at the Emporium cafeteria (back when department stores had restaurants) on Market Street. It was a time of style and elegance. The hippie culture of San Francisco was just beginning and was mostly contained to the infamous Haight-Ashbury district. It was the San Francisco depicted in movies and TV shows of the late 1950s and early 1960s—ladies in nice dresses and gentlemen in suits and ties, even to go to a baseball game or Christmas shopping.

During his family's 1966 Christmas trip, Craig came across a book at Macy's on the presidents of the United States. He was immediately enthralled. While most boys his age wanted a bicycle or BB gun, Craig wanted that book. His parents bought it for him for Christmas, and Craig devoured every page, memorizing the names and dates of all the presidents then shocking his teacher when, at the age of six, he could recite them all in order.

In the following years, Craig read practically everything he could get his hands on about American history, whether it was books on the signers of the Declaration of Independence, presidential First Ladies, the Pilgrims, or other American historical topics. He devoured them all and still has them to this day. When he reached fifth grade, his teacher had to ask him to quit answering all the history questions, so the rest of the class would have a chance.

But when he entered middle school in the early 1970s, Craig started to notice the history curriculum was changing. At first these changes were subtle, but then he noticed a sharp leftward turn in the way his teachers talked about American history. No one told the narrative he fell in love with anymore. In the stories he heard in middle school, high school, and beyond, the men and women he read about as heroes were now villains. The history and heritage Craig was previously taught to be proud of was now depicted as something to be ashamed of. Instead of "My Country 'Tis of Thee," he and his classmates were now singing "If I Had a Hammer."

By the mid-1970s, when Craig got to ninth grade, his world history teacher had portraits of Vladimir Lenin and Mao Zedong hanging in the classroom. This teacher taught students that while these two men may have occasionally been misguided, they were fundamentally benevolent leaders who brought about transformative change in their societies. This teacher completely ignored the reality of Lenin's Russia and Mao's China, where hundreds of millions of people were tortured, imprisoned, and in many cases, slaughtered to bring about these changes.

Thankfully, Hitler was still evil in this teacher's view, but that was one of the few historical realities that made it into the curriculum. This teacher asserted that Americans were lied to by their leaders for generations, such as our country's motives in opposing the Soviet Union and Communist China—stating it was all about money instead of freedom.

He also taught as fact all sorts of conspiracy theories, particularly about the John F. Kennedy assassination—all to impressionable students who simply did not have the training and the grounding to discern the truth. Craig was able to withstand the brainwashing. Unfortunately, many of his peers were not.

When Craig entered college in the late 1970s, things were even worse. One of his professors told his sophomore history class he openly taught revisionist history and would be telling them about the "true" (at least in his eyes) story of America. In this professor's view, America was responsible for the Cold War because it refused to bow to the "reasonable" demands of the Soviet Union.

The new narrative always questioned America's motives while never questioning the Soviet Union's. It overlooked the USSR's brutal oppression of Eastern Europe and, against all evidence, glorified nightmarish regimes like Mao's. In this new narrative, America was always guilty. To maintain this illusion, the progressive historical narrative had to sweep the heinous crimes of Castro, Che, Pol Pot, and other Marxist leaders under the rug.

Ignoring evil for the sake of a narrative is always dangerous—that is a lesson history has shown time and time again.

Craig knew America as a country was far from perfect because none of us are perfect. As a child of the 1960s and 1970s, he was keenly aware of the sin of racism, a dark stain on America's legacy. He watched the assassination of Rev. Dr. Martin Luther King Jr. on television and saw the vile actions of those who celebrated his death. He also read the words of past Americans, who managed to condemn racism and other evils without denigrating America's good qualities. But in the narrative presented by his progressive teachers, there was no self-awareness, no exploration of the goods and evils of various regimes. There was only one story: America was evil, and her enemies—the Soviet Union, Maoist China, Castro's Cuba, Pol Pot's Cambodia—were either victims of American aggression or started with good intentions but became misguided somewhere along the way.

Nothing is that simple. Craig saw this narrative take a terrible toll on his classmates. They became cynical, jaded, and disrespectful toward their own country and heritage while at the same time becoming completely uncritical of other regimes. They lost the ability to have civil discourse about topics and instead took completely black-and-white stances on complicated issues. And eventually, they denounced anyone who disagreed with them as ignorant, or even evil, as they parroted back what they were being taught.

I had a totally different experience—at least until I got to college. Indiana was far behind California in adopting this revisionist narrative of American history, so I received a traditional history and civics education all the way through high school.

But when I entered Indiana University, I received a full dose of what Craig experienced in northern California. For instance, I was told the Pilgrims were European oppressors who destroyed Native American culture. My professors denied the Pilgrims were fleeing religious persecution when they made the dangerous and, in some cases, deadly voyage across the Atlantic in the Mayflower. Instead, my professors said, the Pilgrims were persecutors who engaged in cultural genocide.

My professors also clearly believed American descendants of European immigrants needed to apologize for our forefathers coming to these shores in the first place. They also believed Americans ought to be apologetic about the Judeo-Christian principles the Puritans and many other European immigrants brought with them, as these principles are now seen as oppressive and intolerant.

Like Craig's, my professors refused to engage in a good-faith discussion about the profound role these Judeo-Christian beliefs have played in urging governments to protect freedom and human dignity for all people. Instead, they insisted everything the early European settlers of America did was evil—including the Mayflower Compact, which upheld freedom in a new and vital way (I will discuss the role of the Mayflower Compact in America's founding in a later chapter).

Since then, this view has come to dominate our civil discourse, and few people dare to speak up against it unless they wish to be mocked, ridiculed, and in modern terms, "cancelled."

When I first heard this false narrative, I could not help but think of my paternal grandfather who immigrated legally to the United States from Macedonia in 1916, entering—as so many did—through Ellis Island.

My grandfather loved his new home and believed the United States of America was the greatest country in the world. His own love of country, grounded in his own immigrant experience, helped instill that same love of country in my own life and heart. He could compare the circumstances he came from with what he experienced in America, and that comparison made him appreciate America even more.

That sense of patriotism inspired the Greatest Generation, many of whom were first- and second-generation immigrants, to fight against fascism in World War II; they knew what was at stake. They did not take their freedom for granted, and they were willing to make the ultimate sacrifice to defend that freedom.

The narrative infecting our education system today is having the opposite effect: rather than uniting Americans from diverse backgrounds and cultures around a shared love, it is dividing us and spreading hatred.

The result of this narrative is America no longer being a melting pot but an overboiling kettle of warring tribes pitted against each other in a zero-sum battle over whose "rights" can trump the others'. We have completely forgotten rights imply responsibilities and a shared duty to each other. Dip one dissenting toe in this kettle, and it quickly becomes a pool of piranhas, ready to strip you to the bone in seconds. Our "more perfect union" has been shattered.

## LIBERALS AND CONSERVATIVES AGREE

In 1991, liberal historian Arthur Schlesinger Jr. recognized the danger threatening American culture after he reviewed a New York state report calling for K-12 curricula to address "racial and ethnic oppression" and focus on group identities instead of a collective culture. Schlesinger rightly pointed out that individual freedom and political democracy are essential elements of who we are as Americans. These two attributes, if not undergirded by a strong set of shared values, can lead to social fragmentation. Therefore, Americans must be diligent in protecting and promoting the things that unite us, rather than fixating on what divides us. Schlesinger warned how fixating on the things dividing us would shatter our educational institutions into war zones, groups pitted against each other with no sense of collective identity.[3]

Schlesinger was prophetic. Americans no longer share a hope for the future and a sense of the common good. Instead, young people leave our education system cynical, entitled, and aggrieved. Rather than being thankful, they are indignant. Rather than proud, they feel ashamed. Rather than feeling free, they feel oppressed. Rather than wanting to fix America's faults, they want to burn America down. Rather than asking what they can do for their country, they demand to know what their country can do for them—and the answer is increasingly to "cease to exist."

I had the opportunity during my time at the White House to spend an afternoon with Mr. Schlesinger in his Manhattan home. One of the topics of our conversation was the fragmenting of America.

Even though he is a man of the Left, and I am a man of the Right, we found we share a common interest in maintaining national unity. We have differences, but we recognize we have a common bond. We both believe America has a strong foundation and vast potential to protect freedom, rights, and human dignity for millions of people. We believe America has raised the standard for the rest of the world for prosperity, peace, and freedom. One of us may walk the Left road and the other the Right road, but we have a shared destination: the best our country can be, based in love of that country.

That afternoon, I told Mr. Schlesinger his writings were prophetic in their declaration of the coming historic and cultural battles. These battles are now in full force, dividing our land.

Many young people are not being taught even the most basic information, resulting in a citizenry divorced both intellectually and emotionally from its heritage. In today's schools, students are told what to think instead of how to think. Now, instead of truth, students are taught "interpretations." But as one friend of mine, Bobb Biehl, says, "Nothing has meaning without context."

John De Gree, the founder of The Classical Historian,[4] a website seeking to teach children a balanced view of history, says, "Instead of learning history content and the thinking and rhetorical skills of the historian, students in most schools are indoctrinated to memorize a certain version of the past and are dissuaded from learning how to think for themselves."[5]

The ramifications of this indoctrination go far beyond the history curriculum. When the American educational system began to fall alarmingly behind other industrialized nations in math and science, either landing in the middle of the pack or lower in international exams, schools started placing a greater emphasis on these subjects and neglected history, civics, literature, and language arts.

Unfortunately, schools do not recognize education is a holistic process; discouraging clear thinking in one subject undermines clear thinking in every other subject. The new emphasis on math and science has barely moved the needle for U.S. students in those subjects[6] because the alarming test numbers are a result of systemic failures, not subject-specific ones. But it has had quite the negative result of deflecting attention from the failures of historical and civic education for young Americans.

Even if students escape high school with some semblance of a grounding in history and civics, they are virtually guaranteed to receive an onslaught of anti-America venom once they enter college. I am not the only one saying this. People from both sides of the political spectrum are raising the alarm.

William Galston, former domestic policy advisor to President Clinton, said in the *Wall Street Journal*: "Consider the formative experiences of adults 30 and younger. For them, the Cold War exists only in history books—which they didn't necessarily read. High schools in only 31 states require a year-long U.S. history class . . . . Against this backdrop, it isn't hard to understand why only 15% of those under 30 think the U.S. is the greatest nation on earth, why nearly half believe hard work is no guarantor of success, or why so many of them support a single national health-care program."[7]

Algis Valiunas, writing for the conservative American Enterprise Institute, vividly describes the narrative most young people receive:

> The honorable opposition may be gallant and spirited (and not incidentally have truth on its side), but it is losing: the American story most countrymen tell themselves is fast becoming one of an illegitimate founding, systemic race-based hatred, irremediable wrongdoing on the part of once-revered statesmen and soldiers, economic exploitation of the many by the few, and the raving of once-pristine nature by businessmen heedless of any good but their own profit. America, in sum, with little to be proud of and everything to its shame, has habitually violated the tenets of its political creed—its professed belief in freedom and equality—and never possessed rightful title to its vaunted exceptionalism, which amounts to so much hypocrisy and braggadocio. Not only are we not better than most people, we are, in fact, among the worst. The sooner we are all made to realize our own viciousness and inherited guilt, the better off we will be.[8]

Andrew Michta, dean of the College of International and Security Studies at the George C. Marshall European Center for Security Studies in Garmisch-Partenkirchen, Germany, echoes these concerns. He writes that America is in the grip of a cultural revolution. This revolution, he says, was decades in the making. It was born in our colleges and universities, which have equipped the "shock troops" leading the charge. These "shock troops" are now toppling statues of our nation's founders, removing monuments to presidents, renaming schools, censoring speech, and redrafting curricula. He writes,

> They do so because they fervently believe that they are better than their hopelessly retrograde fellow citizens, who remain blind or, worse, callously indifferent to the alleged ills that plague our society. College and university campuses across the country have been transformed by leftist faculty into seminaries that each year anoint into the "woke priesthood" more credentialed but hardly educated men and women.
>
> The religion of wokeness taught in our schools and preached in most realms of American life rests on a mutated strand of Marxism, only this time it is not the oppressed proletariat that is to be freed by the party elite and given the "correct" consciousness. . . .
>
> The result? Arguably the greatest fracturing of our national fabric since the Civil War, one that has made it nearly impossible for many Gen Z and American millennials to concede that their opponents—which is to say the rest of society— even deserve to participate in our democracy. The other side is not merely misguided but increasingly illegitimate.[9]

## How Historical and Civic Ignorance Influences America's Youth

This indoctrination at the university level shows up in numerous surveys. For instance, just before the Fourth of July 2020, the Young America's Foundation and *Townhall.com* released a poll showing the toll the attacks on America's history and heritage have taken on college students. In comparing the views of college students to high school students, the pollsters found:

- 88% of high schoolers view the U.S. favorably compared to 69% of college students,
- 91% of high schoolers view the U.S. flag favorably compared to 73% of college students,
- 63% of high schoolers are proud of the U.S. compared to only 40% of college students,
- 58% of high schoolers say they are patriotic compared to just 35% of college students,
- 85% of high schoolers say they are glad to live in the U.S. compared to 73% of college students, and
- 48% of high schoolers would sacrifice for America compared to a paltry 32% of college students.[10]

This makes sense. After all, who would want to fight to protect a country one despises? Who would try to defend a nation one has been told over and over is evil?

Another 2021 poll from *Issues & Insights* revealed only 36 percent of adults aged eighteen and twenty-four said they were "proud to be American," compared with 86 percent of those over the age of sixty-five. Conservative commentator Ben Shapiro said, "This shouldn't be surprising. America's children have been raised in a system dedicated to the proposition that America itself is evil, a repository of discrimination and bigotry, a country founded in sin and steeped in cruelty."[11]

In *The Public Discourse*, I came across a piece by Jeremy Adams, a teacher, describing this mindset succinctly, as he observed a shift in America's youth over the years from an attitude of gratitude to one of ingratitude in almost every area—toward their parents, their teachers, and toward society as a whole. He wrote, "My real concern is that gratitude may no longer be part of the lives of young Americans. They seem to believe their blessings . . . bountiful freedom, and opportunities unrivaled in human history—are owed to them. They see no need to be grateful; it makes no sense to them. The decline of gratitude portends a disturbing pivot in our culture. I worry not that my own world may be crumbling, not that civilization's decline is imminent, but that unless the younger generation learns the virtue of gratitude, they will not find joy in life."[12]

When children learn America was supposedly founded on a "lie," their parents are wrong about everything, and the government will provide everything they need without having to earn it; this sense of personal entitlement and ingratitude grows like a cancerous tumor on their souls. This lack of gratitude is a poison that infects everything—from patriotism to personal relationships.

But that is exactly what they are being taught in the present American classroom and culture. The result is a fragmented America—child vs. parent, young vs. old, rich vs. poor, race vs. race, etc., with each looking out for their self-interests, rather than the greater interest of others and the nation.

That is why I felt compelled to write this book: to bring awareness to the problem and to warn my fellow citizens about the dangers of sacrificing our heritage to those who seek to radically transform America. The lack of teaching history, or teaching a distorted view of history, impacts every aspect of our lives: from our civil discourse to our economy to our most basic freedoms, such as freedom of religion and freedom of speech.

But I do not just want to identify the problem and despair. It is essential we have a solution and convey hope for the future.

That solution is viral, like so many other things today, meaning it starts with talking with our children, then with our friends and neighbors, and then with teachers—and always in a civil manner based on mutual respect. Just like the cancer of ignorance and disinformation spreads from one person to another, from one region to another, we must reverse the trend and spread a message that accurately portrays our nation's history and heritage.

This message will hopefully restore America, one person at a time. It has the potential to restore our country as one nation, united in purpose, regardless our political, economic, and religious differences. That is what I propose, and that is what will restore hope for us all.

# 1

# *"Don't Know Much About History"*

*The diffusion of knowledge is the only guardian of true liberty. . . . [I]t is universally admitted that a well-instructed people alone can permanently be a free people.*[1]

JAMES MADISON

*One of our greatest national dangers is ignorance of America's profound legacy of freedom. I firmly believe that ignorance is a threat to freedom.*[2]

DR. PETER LILLBACK

*Before the outrageous assault on the U.S. Capitol, before the rancor of the 2020 presidential election, before the mob violence that engulfed cities across our nation . . . long before all this, Americans had been engaged in a fierce struggle over the history, meaning, and future of the United States. The American Founders, it is worth recalling, faced an even more fearsome challenge: to bring together different views and competing factions to build a unified, federal, and democratic republic.*[3]

JOSEPH LOCONTE

~~~

A while back, I came across an interesting, and disturbing, article written by the personal physician to David McCullough, a noted historian and author. The article was entitled, "What's Keeping David McCullough from Sleeping."

McCullough is the award-winning author of books on Harry S. Truman, John Adams, the building of the Panama Canal, and many other historical leaders and events. He has received several of the top English-language literature awards, including the Pulitzer Prize (twice) and the National Book Award, and he is also a recipient of the National Medal of Freedom.

Now in his eighties, McCullough came to his doctor complaining of insomnia, a common issue with people in his age group. When his physician asked McCullough what was keeping him up at night, he responded, "I have to tell you—part of it is worrying about what is happening in our country."[4]

Writing about the conversation, his physician says, "Every day, as [McCullough] reads the papers, it seems as if leaders are taking positions based on politics—and have forgotten about history. They are unaware of the past, and uninterested in how they will be remembered in the future."[5]

This should be keeping us all up at night, not just David McCullough. This disregard of history from the leading voices of our time is the result of decades of neglect of history and civics at all levels of our educational system.

Like Mr. Schlesinger who I mentioned earlier, I had the honor of also meeting with Mr. McCullough twice when I served in the White House. During one of those meetings, we had an extensive conversation about his deep concern about America's illiteracy, a concern that has only deepened within him over the succeeding years.

And if it is taught, as mentioned earlier, the version of history communicated greatly distorts and defames the motives and truth about those who shaped our country, resulting in Americans pitted against each other, rather than living together in harmony. As a result, our very republic becomes increasingly wobbly as it struggles to remain standing while lurching from one cultural crisis to another.

The problem extends far beyond our leaders. Survey after depressing survey documents how woefully uninformed American citizens are about our nation's history and freedoms.

For example, a 2009 survey of Oklahoma public high school students found, when faced with ten questions drawn from the U.S. citizenship test all legal immigrants must take to become citizens, students floundered. Only one in four could correctly name George Washington as the first president of the United States. Only 10 percent of students knew there are nine justices on the Supreme Court, and only 29 percent knew the president headed the executive branch of government. *Only 3 percent* of students were able to answer six out of the ten questions—the passing score for the U.S. citizenship test.[6]

These high school students from 2009 are now entering their thirties. They are casting votes, rallying, and even running for and holding political office—all without having even a basic grasp of how our system of government works.

This is not a new problem. A 2008 study by the Intercollegiate Studies Institute (ISI) surveyed more than 2,500 Americans and found only half of adults could name the three branches of government. Only 36 percent of college graduates could do so.[7] Eighteen percent of students tested could not name a single right or freedom guaranteed under the First Amendment, and only 54 percent could correctly define free enterprise as a system in which individuals create, exchange, and control goods and services.[8] The highest performing school on the civics test administered by ISI was Harvard University, the so-called gold standard of America academia. Harvard scored 69.56 percent—a D+, a failing grade.[9]

Another survey from 2009, this one conducted by the American Revolution Center, found more Americans could correctly identify Michael Jackson as the singer of the songs "Beat It" and "Billie Jean" than could identify the Bill of Rights as part of the U.S. Constitution. In addition, more than half of the people surveyed attributed the quote, "From each according to his ability, to each according to his needs," to George Washington, Thomas Paine, or then-president Barack Obama. It is in fact a quote from Karl Marx, the author of *The Communist Manifesto*.[10]

Josiah Bunting of the National Civic Literary Board said of the survey, "This [. . .] provides stark evidence that American citizens of the 21st century are increasingly—sadly, deplorably—ignorant of their legacy, their political and con-stitutional birthright of the 18th century."[11]

Ten years later, things have not improved. A 2018 survey done by the Woodrow Wilson National Fellowship Founda-tion investigated the civic and historical knowledge of people in all fifty states and found only 53 percent were able to earn a passing grade in U.S. history. Eighty-five percent could not identify the year the U.S. Constitution was written. Even more alarmingly, one in four people did not know freedom of speech was guaranteed under the U.S. Constitution.[12]

Ignorance is not confined to civics—it extends to history as well. Seventy-two percent of those surveyed did not know which states comprised the original thirteen colonies; 37 per-cent believed Benjamin Franklin invented the light bulb; only

24 percent knew colonists fought the Revolutionary War over unjust taxation; and 12 percent believed Dwight Eisenhower led the military in the American Civil War (thirty years before he was born!). Finally, while most managed to identify the cause of the Cold War, 2 percent said climate change caused the Cold War![13]

While one may ask, "Does it really affect someone's day-to-day life if she knows whether Thomas Edison (the correct answer) or Benjamin Franklin invented the light bulb?," the truth is ignorance of history—including historical details—is isolating. When we do not know the stories behind the things that make up our daily lives—things as disparate and dear to our society as light bulbs, the American flag, the interstate highway system, freedom of speech and association—we forget what labor and effort those things cost our forebears. We do not value them. And when we cease to value things, we stand to lose them.

But sadly, such ignorance is pervasive. In 2017, David Fouse, writing in *National Review*, reported the American Council of Trustees and Alumni found half of all college graduates did not know how long the terms of their representatives and senators were and 43 percent did not know the First Amendment gave them freedom of speech. A full third could not identify any rights guaranteed by the First Amendment.[14] This is not surprising, as Fouse reports, because in a survey of more than one thousand liberal arts colleges, only 18 percent included a course in U.S. history or government as part of their graduation requirement.[15]

There is also a push to exclude military history; whereas 85 percent of history departments used to include a war or diplomatic historian, now less than half feature such a scholar.[16] Tami Davis Biddle, who teaches at the U.S. Army War

College, says the decline in war studies and military history in U.S. universities has come about because, "Unfortunately, many in the academic community assume that military history is simply about powerful men—mainly white men—fighting each other and/or oppressing vulnerable groups."[17]

Biddle urges faculty and students alike to put aside this false assumption for the good of society. She writes, "Military history ought to be a vital component of a liberal education, one that prepares students to be informed and responsible citizens."[18] How can we possibly hope to avoid wars in the future—or, if necessary, win wars thrust upon us by enemies—if we do not know anything about the wars of our past?

Even when students can study history or civics, the education is paltry. A RAND Corporation survey from 2019 found just 32 percent of K-12 teachers considered "knowledge of facts"—such as of the American Revolution—to be "absolutely essential" to social studies, dead last on a list of twelve other items including being "tolerant of people and groups who are different from themselves" and "activists who challenge the status quo."[19] In 2020, RAND found most social studies teachers felt they were not "well prepared to support students' civic development."[20] At least teachers are aware of their own shortcomings in teaching history and civics.

## The Consequences of Historical Ignorance

We are now several decades deep in this mire of historical and civic ignorance, and we are beginning to see the political and social ramifications. Our elected leaders no longer know the basics of the government they work within.

For instance, New York Congresswoman Alexandria Ocasio-Cortez, seen as an enlightened heroine by progressives and their allies in the media, could not name the three branches of government (executive, legislative, and judicial) when asked in an interview. She incorrectly said that the three branches of the federal government are the White House, the Senate, and the House of Representatives.[21] This is a member of Congress, who does not even know the basics of the Constitution she has sworn to protect!

The same ISI study that gave Harvard a D+ in civics studies also surveyed elected officials and made some distressing discoveries. Thirty percent of *elected officials* did not know the phrase "life, liberty, and the pursuit of happiness" comes from the Declaration of Independence.[22] Forty-three percent had no idea how the Electoral College worked, with one in five claiming it trained "those aspiring for higher political office" or "was established to supervise the first televised presidential debates."[23] I wouldn't be surprised if one of these elected officials tried to place a bet on the electoral college's football team.

This collective ignorance has led to a collapse of civil discourse. We have no shared language, which makes it impossible to have meaningful discussions about difficult topics. The loss of shared language is so complete many Americans either do not recognize or do not appreciate the words of our founding documents—words, regardless how well they have been implemented, that represent a new standard for human rights and political dignity.

In 2017, when National Public Radio tweeted out the text of the Declaration of Independence on the Fourth of July, 140 characters at a time, Jonah Goldberg reported they received comments such as "Are you drunk?" and "Glad you're being defunded, your show was never balanced."[24] These derisive words came from people on the Left and on the Right alike. Our whole political spectrum is plagued by ignorance.

In *The Life of Reason*, a sweeping study of how human imagination and reason work together to bring order from chaos, the philosopher George Santayana wrote one of his most famous lines: "Those who can't remember the past are doomed to repeat it."[25] Santayana recognizes that a historical sense—a grounding in what has come before—is essential, both on an individual level and on a societal level, to bring civilization and order from the chaos of our perceptions and passions. If we have no historical sense, we are swept along by events and dominated by our reactions to those events. We cannot view events in context; we cannot balance our perceptions with awareness of what may be happening beyond our perceptions. And as a result, we get caught in the same vicious cycles that have brought down civilizations for the past ten thousand years.

That is exactly what is happening in America: we are repeating the mistakes of other great civilizations that collapsed from within. As Jarrett Stepman of the Heritage Foundation warns: "We don't want to be trapped by the past, but we do want to learn from it in order to avoid repeating past mistakes and build a better future. As citizens, knowledge of the past and of civics is crucial. Lacking such knowledge is unhealthy for a free country, and even dangerous, given how bad political life can become."[26]

He then brings up another issue that will be the main focus of this book, writing, "One of the biggest problems today is that we often focus on tearing down our history rather than learning from it."[27] His statement is a perfect description of the current state of domestic affairs.

David Fouse concurs:

> As shocking as [these] statistics are, they represent only the surface of the problem. What we are facing is not merely a crisis of knowledge, a need to memorize more facts, or a lack of understanding of how to properly engage. What we are really facing is a crisis of worldview. . . . A government by the people, for the people, and of the people is only as wise, as just, and as free as the people themselves. . . . Ignorance and indifference eventually erode our freedoms and destroy our republic. It is not without cause that our national discourse in recent years has become so histrionic and hateful.[28]

He concludes, "It is this knowledge that makes self-governance possible. It is this knowledge that made us the freest nation in the world. It is this knowledge that will maintain our freedoms. All the government money, programs, and agencies in the world cannot teach this knowledge."[29]

As these individuals have pointed out, one of the main causes in the deterioration of our national discourse has been the decline in the teaching of history and civics, or when it is taught, it is done so in a distorted manner. Nature abhors a vacuum. In the absence of civics and history education, radical activists are using that space to indoctrinate our children into their dangerous worldview.

When there is no historical context to draw upon, no shared history, and no understanding of how government works, it becomes seed to sow division and discord in hearts and minds. When people are not equipped to refute an argument and lack the critical thinking skills to see beyond the rhetoric, they tend to accept it at face value. They become easy prey for demagogues—from the Left and the Right alike. They become tools to be exploited for a certain agenda.

Throw into this mix social media, which enables personal opinions, on the Left and the Right, to be perceived as facts and misinformation to spread to an ignorant populace, and suddenly we're all drinking a toxic brew dividing our nation into various tribes all pitted against each other in a zero-sum game. There is no room of civilized disagreement.

A lack of knowledge, combined with overheated discourse, leads to a lack of nuance, empathy, and a mindset that everyone is guilty until proven innocent and can only be proven innocent based on the terms of the tribe—whether it is a tribe on the Left or the Right.

That is the opposite of the way American jurisprudence was structured. Due process, for the most part, no longer exists in the hearts and minds of the American public. People believe if you do not agree with them, you are guilty of perpetuating "systemic injustice," and justice demands you be silenced. You must be cancelled: not allowed to speak your mind on any topic until the ruling tribe decrees you have appropriately repented of your alleged sins and are no longer cancelled.

This mindset has led to mobs destroying or defacing statues, activists rewriting history to fit the narratives of the various tribes, a mob storming the U.S. Capitol to overturn an election, and public figures vilifying patriotism and national pride.

Instead of celebrating our freedoms and working together to solve our problems, our current culture is tying us up in rhetorical straitjackets where only one form of thought is allowed and all other forms are mocked, shamed, and even criminalized. Our historical ignorance is leading us to deny and suppress the freedoms upon which our nation was founded.

If our republic is going to survive, we must encourage robust debate, not discourage it. The ability to freely discuss issues from different perspectives is a crucial sign of a healthy and vibrant society. But a robust debate requires both sides to be fully engaged and equipped with the historical and logical arguments to make their case. When one side—or both—has no historical or logical arguments, and only bases their views on emotion, there can be no debate. Without a debate, a society starts an accelerating slide into chaos. And in our society, one side is often not even allowed to speak in the first place.

No wonder David McCullough suffers from insomnia. All this causes some sleepless nights for me as well. I cannot help but hear the prophetic words of President Dwight Eisenhower from his 1953 inaugural address and realize they increasingly ring true: *A people that values its privileges above its principles, soon loses both.*[30] We have forgotten our principles while exalting our privileges, but without principles to serve as a foundation, we will eventually lose our privileges.

That is what we are seeing playing out in our culture every day.

## THE SUMMER OF 2020

We had a perfect example of how this played out from the summer of 2020. After police confrontations in various cities left several Blacks dead, radical Left-wing mobs seized upon the tragedies to riot, destroying small businesses, vandalizing stores and public streets, and burning police vehicles. They also continued an ongoing campaign of vandalizing or toppling historical statues and monuments. On a more frightening scale, the "woke" Left exerted immense pressure against these historical symbols, forcing public officials to remove them and erase the memories of those who founded America or played important roles in our history—without any knowledge of that history.

This mob warfare against our past has gone far beyond the symbols of the Old Confederacy to include memorials of those who stood against injustice. For instance, rioters in northern California toppled a statue of Ulysses S. Grant, the military leader who led the anti-slavery North to victory in the American Civil War.[31]

Grant led postwar efforts to provide and protect civil rights, such as the right to vote, for recently freed Black Americans. He signed legislation to clamp down on white-supremacist terrorism in the South.

At his funeral, Grant was eulogized by Black antislavery leader Frederick Douglass, who said Grant was, "a man too broad for prejudice, too humane to despise the humblest, too great to be small at any point. In him the Negro found a protector, the Indian a friend, a vanquished foe a brother, an imperiled nation a savior."[32]

But because at one point Grant was "gifted" a slave— whom he quickly freed because he believed slavery to be repugnant—he must be erased from history, even though history shows he devoted much of his life to ending slavery and protecting the rights of Black Americans.

Mobs toppled or vandalized statues of Francis Scott Key, the writer of the Star-Spangled Banner,[33] and Father Junipero Serra, founder of the California missions in the 1700s who worked for racial reconciliation and spoke out in defense of Native Americans.[34]

Protestors in Philadelphia damaged a statue of Matthias Baldwin, who fought for the abolition of slavery, founded a school for Black children, and advocated for Blacks to have the right to vote—all in the early 1800s, well before the Civil War.[35] In Boston, vandals attacked the monument commemorating the 34th Regiment, the first volunteer all-Black Civil War regiment, which was commanded by abolitionist and equal-rights champion Robert Gould Shaw.[36]

Succumbing to intense pressure, the New York Museum of National History removed a statue of Theodore Roosevelt. The statue depicts Roosevelt sitting on a horse with a Native American and Black on either side, which critics say further a narrative of racism and colonization.[37]

Vandals defaced the statue of Winston Churchill in London on D-Day,[38] some of whom admitted they were totally ignorant of the fact Churchill helped lead the Allies in stopping Adolf Hitler—and his genocide of European Jews.

And, of course, statues of George Washington, Thomas Jefferson, Abraham Lincoln, and Theodore Roosevelt[39] have been also targeted across the country by vandals and public officials.

It seems like we should soon expect elected officials to take dynamite to Mt. Rushmore!

*Now, I want to assert that I am a Lincoln* man and a Christian who firmly believes all people are made in the image of God—*imago Dei*—and deserve utmost dignity and respect. The truth is disdain for human dignity—toward various groups—was America's original sin. Its stain continues to mar our nation more than 150 years after the Emancipation Proclamation was signed by Abraham Lincoln and the North was victorious in the Civil War.

Americans of color continue to struggle to receive equal opportunities in many ways, for a huge variety of reasons. Many of these struggles are tied to the breakdown of the family caused by governmental policies that have harmed, rather than helped, their ability to rise from poverty. As a Christian, I see this is a deep problem and one all Americans must work together to resolve. No one should feel as if he or she is less significant or less valuable because of the color of his or her skin.

Indiscriminately destroying our history will not bring justice to our future. This dismantlement of history strips us of the models we can look to for encouragement and inspiration moving forward. Remember the Ulysses S. Grant statue I wrote about earlier? Grant dedicated his life to two things: unifying America and righting racial injustices. Should he be erased because he, by the fact of his existence, was implicated however briefly in the evil system he sought to end? Or should we look to him as an example of how to respond to evil systems: with force and courage, bringing all our energy to bear to bring justice whenever and wherever we can? Grant went out and physically labored in the fields alongside his father-in-law's slaves, seeking to understand them. He freed the one slave he was given. Throughout his life, he became more and more stalwart on the issue of racial equality and justice.[40]

This is not a story we should erase—rather, it is one we should magnify, because it shows each of us how to respond to injustice and evil. Erasing this story leaves us helpless and divided, with fewer ideas of how to bring peace and justice.

When, in a misguided attempt to erase evil, we erase history, we give evil a stronger hold. This is because history—the good and the bad—is what gives us a sense of meaning and of direction. We look to history to understand where we are today; our cultural and social wounds make no sense without history. Without knowing where those wounds came from, we have no hope of healing them. Instead, we face fragmentation and division in a fractured, meaningless society.

The dismantling and destruction of statues and monuments we are witnessing is symbolic of the dismantling of meaning. Instead of *e pluribus Unum* ("out of many, one"), we have become the exact opposite: we're destroying our only chance of unity and allowing individual whims to trump collective good. Instead of a nation, we are disintegrating into a conglomerate of tribes warring with each other to protect selfish interests.

What is fueling this movement is "critical race theory," which I will discuss throughout this book. But to understand this so-called movement, it needs to be defined first.

The best explanation of critical race theory I have read came from Christopher Rufo, founder and director of Battlefront, a public policy research center devoted to refuting it. In a lecture at Hillsdale College, he said, "In explaining critical race theory, it helps to begin with a brief history of Marxism. Originally, the Marxist Left built its political program on the theory of class conflict. Marx believed that the primary characteristic of industrial societies was the imbalance of power between capitalists and workers. The solution to that imbalance, according to Marx, was revolution: the workers would eventually gain consciousness of their plight, seize the means of production, overthrow the capitalist class, and usher in a new socialist society."[41]

Thus, critical race theory is the latest salvo by the far Left to deceive and divide Americans to achieve their ultimate goal of a socialist society. Rufo continues, "During the 20th century, a number of regimes underwent Marxist-style revolutions, and each ended in disaster. Socialist governments in the Soviet Union, China, Cambodia, Cuba, and elsewhere racked up a body count of nearly 100 million of their own people. They are remembered for their gulags, show trials, executions, and mass starvations. In practice, Marx's ideas unleashed man's darkest brutalities."[42]

He goes on to state, Western Marxists came to the realization "workers revolutions" would not work in countries with a much higher standard of living. Therefore, to achieve their dream of socialism, they had to create divisions by class and race. That led to the creation of critical race theory, created in the 1990s, which Rufo says was built on the intellectual framework of identity-based Marxism. While ignored by the greater culture for several decades, it slowly became injected into government agencies, public school systems, teacher training programs, and corporate human resources departments in the form of diversity training programs, human resources modules, public policy frameworks, and school curricula.[43] All this was designed to turn Americans against each other, and especially against the principle of ordered liberty upon which our country was founded.

If this movement continues unabated, we will truly become "a house divided against itself."[44] Lincoln spoke those words in his famous 1858 speech before the Republican Convention, and he was quoting Jesus Christ in Mark 3:25. That house divided, Jesus warned, "cannot stand."

## SO, WHAT CAN WE DO?

We cannot stand idly by watching our nation, and what it represents, collapse from within through the destruction of our history and heritage. We must fight for unity. That is the only way we can stand.

To do this will require a proactive approach, rather than a reactive one, and it must start in our homes. Those who seek to erase our history and heritage often advance their agenda through state and federal programs while many Americans are totally unaware this is happening. Too many parents still trust their local public schools to teach history adequately and accurately. They may see problems in other schools but are in denial about what is being taught to their own children. Or they may become aware of what is happening but decide they do not want to rock the boat. For many ordinary Americans, the price of taking on radical activists, especially in the Internet age, is simply too high.

But the boat is full of holes, and it is carrying us to deep and dangerous waters. It not only needs to be rocked; it needs to be flipped over. Right now, we're still in the shallows. We can still wade back to shore. But that will not be true for much longer. The boat is going to go down eventually. If we wait, if we continue to be in denial and to say everything is fine, it will take us and our children down with it.

We can no longer live in denial about what is being taught to our children about our nation's history—as parents are beginning to see with the advancement of critical race theory.

Christopher Rufo shares several examples of how critical race theory is playing out in public schools. He tells about an elementary school in Cupertino, California, that forced first-graders to "deconstruct" their racial and sexual identities, and then rank themselves according to their "power and privilege."

He also shares about how a Springfield, Missouri, middle school forced teachers to locate themselves on an "oppression matrix," which demands straight, white, English-speaking, Christian males must atone for their "privilege" and for engaging in "covert white supremacy."

And, finally, in Philadelphia, an elementary school forced fifth-grade students to celebrate "Black communism" and simulate a Black Power rally to free 1960s radical Angela Davis from prison, where she was once held on charges of murder.[45]

Critical race theory is not a new phenomenon, and it preys upon the historical ignorance of Americans. And while many parents are beginning to awaken to what is being taught, there are still too many who are trusting the public schools to educate their children and are blissfully unaware of the indoctrination they are receiving instead.

Besides speaking out, parents are going to have to go the extra mile to not only educate their children but to equip them to see the agenda behind critical race theory. Thus, if our children are in public schools, we must have regular, intentional conversations with them about the true story of America's founders and founding principles, and how those principles have led to greater freedom and respect for human dignity. These conversations can happen around the dinner table, on family road trips, or when you're out running errands. But they must happen, and they must happen frequently. Children are being told lies every day at school; those lies must be combated every day with truth.

You must know, this will inevitably lead to conflict for your children in the classroom, and you should support them with ardent prayer and unwavering defense.

It is also essential parents review the textbooks and other curriculum being used by their children's schools. It is up to parents to make sure they know what lies their children face.

And parents must also prepare their children to face opposition if they stand up for the truth in their classroom. Thus, as parents, we must educate ourselves accurately on America's history to discern truth from folly.

Equipping your children with an accurate depiction of our nation's history and heritage, given the disinformation or lack of information they are receiving, requires a great deal of effort and time. And sadly, even young Christian men and women are lacking in this area as well.

For more than a decade, my friend Craig worked every summer with Alan Sears to put on two multimedia presentations for conservative Christian law students on four important historical figures: Dwight D. Eisenhower, Ronald Reagan, Margaret Thatcher, and Pope John Paul II. The first presentation on Eisenhower focused on his perseverance and faith and how God prepared him to be the right man at the right time to help lead the Allied victory over Nazi Germany. The second presentation dealt with how Reagan, Thatcher, and John Paul II created an alliance that eventually led to the fall of the Berlin Wall and the Soviet Union.

After these presentations were over, the students filled out evaluations. One message that came across time and time again was these students had not heard these stories before. They never learned the truth about these historical figures in public schools. In fact, many of them heard only the politically correct version of the end of the Soviet Union, in which Mikhail Gorbachev (who *Time* elevated as the 1980s Man of the Decade over Reagan, Thatcher, and John Paul II) was the leader in bringing the tyranny and oppression of the Soviet Union to an end. Even the best and brightest Christian law students were ignorant of history.

Many of these students also remarked how much they enjoyed learning about this history. Some wrote they felt their eyes were opened to the truth.

This is all excellent. But most young people are not going to be fortunate enough to attend elite programs for conservative and Christian law students. Most will never hear anything but the progressive narrative. In other words, most will never hear the truth unless we, as people of faith who love our God-given freedoms and the Judeo-Christian principles upon which our nation was founded, are willing to take the time and energy to educate them.

But since this problem is generational and goes back beyond the current generation of school children to the educational and historical bankruptcy of the past seven decades, we must do the hard work of reeducating ourselves on our history and heritage. We must build our own foundations of knowledge about our country; otherwise, how can we teach the next generation? It is not enough to merely refute disinformation. We must offer true and documented information as an alternative.

Rufo concluded his speech with these words:

> [I]n addition to pointing out the dishonesty of the historical narrative on which critical race theory is predicated, we must promote the true story of America—a story that is honest about injustices in American history, but that places them in the context of our nation's high ideals and the progress we have made towards realizing them. Genuine American history is rich with stories of achievements and sacrifices that will move the hearts of Americans—in

stark contrast to the grim and pessimistic narrative pressed by critical race theorists.

Above all, we must have courage—the fundamental virtue required in our time. Courage to stand and speak the truth. Courage to withstand epithets. Courage to face the mob. Courage to shrug off the scorn of the elites. When enough of us overcome the fear that currently prevents so many from speaking out, the hold of critical race theory will begin to slip. And courage begets courage. It's easy to stop a lone dissenter; it's much harder to stop 10, 20, 100, 1,000, 1,000,000, or more who stand up together for the principles of America. Truth and justice are on our side. If we can muster the courage, we will win.[46]

That is what this book is for: to offer an alternative narrative, one grounded in history and facts, one that does not shy away from the hard truths but also does not go out of its way to destroy and denigrate. I will seek to lay out that foundation, starting with what was bequeathed to us by our nation's founders. We will also look at how that heritage is being destroyed and what is at stake.

# 2

# *Trashing Our Past*

*With each passing year in the classroom, I become more
convinced that there is no such thing as neutral teaching.*[1]

JOSHUA PAULING

*About half the history now taught in schools and colleges is
made windy and barren by the narrow notion of leaving out
the theological theories . . . . Historians seem to have completely
forgotten two facts—First, that men act from ideas; and second,
that it might, therefore, be as well to discover which ideas.*[2]

G. K. CHESTERTON

*In a piddling few decades, the world's most powerful,
influential cultural establishment happened to get demolished
and rebuilt from the ground up. What had basically been a
Christian, patriotic, family-loving, politically moderate part of
society became contemptuous of biblical religion, of patriotism,
of the family, and American greatness. The American cultural
elite used to resemble (more or less) the rest of America. Today it
disdains the rest of America. That's a revolution.*[3]

DAVID GELERNTER

*Popular upheaval, political turmoil, industrial progress—
any combination of these can cause the evolution of a society to*

*leapfrog generations, sweeping aside aspects of the past that might otherwise have lingered for decades. And this must be especially so, when those with newfound power are men who distrust any form of hesitation or nuance, and who prize self-assurance above all.*[4]

AMOR TOWLES

*One of the worst sins of the present—not just ours but any present—is the tendency to condescend toward the past, which is much easier to do when one doesn't trouble to know the full context of that past or try to grasp the nature of its challenges as they presented themselves at the time.*[5]

WILFRED MCCLAY

〜〜〜

Back in 2019, former U.S. Attorney General William Barr gave an extraordinary speech in which he provided one of the most robust defenses of religious freedom in a generation. He said of the increasing and dangerous trend to silence and punish religious faith, "If you rely upon the coercive power of the government to impose restraints [on faith], this will inevitably lead to a government that is too controlling, and you will end up with no liberty, just tyranny."[6]

His remarks could not have come at a more opportune time. Churches and religious organizations, as well as our nation's Judeo-Christian heritage, are coming under more attack now than ever before in our country's history. Politicians now routinely call for the abolition of tax-exempt status for religious organizations, including churches, synagogues, and mosques that do not kneel at the altar of the political

Left. An example of this has occurred with the Biden administration taking power with slim Democratic majorities in the House and Senate and increasing the attacks through legislation such as the "Equality Act," a bill that belies its name, stripping Americans of the religious liberty established in the First Amendment of the U.S. Constitution.

As George Orwell said, "He who controls the language controls politics." Convincing Americans "equality" demands we treat religious individuals and organizations *worse* than others is a masterstroke of language manipulation.

The Equality Act would redefine houses of worship as "public accommodations," lumping them in with football stadiums and shopping malls—an Orwellian twist that ignores religious, and therefore protected, elements of these faith-based organizations. The act states that if a church opens its doors to anyone but its members, it is subject to federal civil rights laws—which the act amends to include sexual orientation and "gender identity."

This would prohibit religious organizations from sharing their beliefs about human sexuality issues, and it would compel them to allow biological men who "identify" as female into female restrooms, showers, and locker rooms (and vice versa).

The Equality Act cements in law a profound misunderstanding of the right to religious freedom protected in the First Amendment. The right guarantees people of *all* faiths—and no faith—will be free to practice their faith, both publicly and privately, without fear of government censorship or coercion. Under the First Amendment, no one should be coerced to go against their conscience. Our nation's founders understood that a society where every person was treated with

*41*

dignity and respect required freedom of religion. When the government feels justified in repressing religion, it feels justified in repressing conscience—and when the government can compel people to violate their conscience, true freedom and true human dignity are impossible.

Unfortunately, Americans no longer understand that sequence: freedom of religion leads to freedom of conscience, which leads to respect for human dignity. They think we can dismantle the foundations—freedom of religion—but leave the building standing—respect for human dignity. Clearly, that is impossible. Once we allow the government to repress and punish people for their religious beliefs, we remove the boundary protecting the individual conscience from government coercion and leave defenseless the whole concept of human dignity.

It is no coincidence even as religious freedom in America comes under fierce attack, we are experiencing an increasing clampdown on personal freedoms and greater governmental control in all aspects of our lives.

For centuries, American leaders have acknowledged the importance of religious liberty in maintaining our other beloved freedoms. For example, both Franklin Roosevelt's famous 1941 "Four Freedoms" speech and John F. Kennedy's remarks on religious freedom when he faced anti-Catholic bigotry spoke to this issue. Roosevelt cited as one of his four freedoms, the "freedom of every person to worship God in his own way—everywhere in the world."[7]

But religious freedom is not merely a passive foundation for other freedoms. It serves as an active check on our worst tendencies—both as individuals and as a society. Attorney General Barr went on to speak about this, saying, "Unless you have an effective restraint, you end up with something dangerous—licentiousness—the unbridled pursuit of personal appetites at the expense of the common good. This is another form of tyranny, where the individual is enslaved by his appetites, and the possibility of healthy community life crumbles.[8]

That statement sums up America in the year 2022. Community life has crumbled, pushing people online to social media to find even a semblance of relationships. But social media is a destructive force magnifying the most extreme voices and permitting people to associate only with the people they already agree with—their "tribe."

In towns and cities, neighbor is pitted against neighbor, and there is no shared purpose to bridge the ideological divide. And everywhere, licentiousness is celebrated: our entire culture sends a message of *if you want it, you are entitled to get it! You do you!* Ubiquitous pornography; socially permitted disposal of "useless" or "inconvenient" individuals through abortion, doctor-assisted suicide, the examples go on and on of how our culture trains us to use, abuse, and dispose of anything—or anyone. Meanwhile, those who try to uphold morality face ridicule and, perhaps soon, criminalization.

Barr went on to say, "In fact, Judeo-Christian moral standards are the ultimate utilitarian rules for human conduct . . . . They are like God's instruction manual for the best running of man and human society."[9]

America's founders knew religious faith plays a vital role in creating and sustaining a self-governing, well-ordered society. Faith made people fit to exercise liberty. This concept is central to all our nation's founding documents.

One of those founders, John Adams knew this to be true, saying in 1798 in an address to the Massachusetts Militia, "Our Constitution was made only for a moral and religious people. It is wholly inadequate to the government of any other."[10] Without the moral goalposts religion provides, liberty becomes licentiousness, and regard for human dignity is replaced by the elevation of self.

The founders understood that removing religious freedom in a society creates a vacuum tyranny and oppression will fill. History has proven John Adams correct: When people abandon a moral or righteous foundation, societies collapse. The foundation may still be in place, but the building atop it has become rotten and, thus, becomes easy to topple as soon as the winds start to blow.

Many of the ills we presently face as a nation—incivility, broken families, drug abuse, urban violence—are the manifestations of this. We have replaced the blueprint bequeathed us through the Declaration of Independence and the Constitution with a blank document each person is told to fill in for himself or herself.

The contemporary hatred of religious morality is so intense people are willing to dig the foundations out from under their own feet. They are willing to defame goodness, truth, and beauty simply because it is associated with religion—even if that means all they have left is evil, lies, and ugliness.

This is what happened to Father Junipero Serra. His legacy has been rewritten by far-Left historians and activists who turned him from a benevolent servant into a spiritual version of Simon Legree, the villain of *Uncle Tom's Cabin*, for one reason only: Father Serra was a devout Christian and Spanish Franciscan monk—so devout Pope Francis canonized him as a saint in 2015.

My friend Craig has a personal love of Father Junipero Serra. Back in the late 1960s, when he was growing up in northern California, Craig and his classmates spent an entire semester learning California history—particularly about the California missions. Father Serra founded nine of these missions, including the first one in San Diego.

Even though he and his family were not Catholic, Craig was fascinated by the story of Father Serra. He pleaded with his parents to take him on a trip to visit some of the missions Father Serra founded, which they did. Craig fell especially in love with Mission San Juan Bautista, located about an hour south of San Francisco. The mission, which was made famous in the Alfred Hitchcock movie *Vertigo*, includes a charming pioneer town where visitors can wander around and soak in what it must have been like in the early days of California. Another favorite was Mission San Juan Capistrano in southern California, with its famous swallows greeting visitors to the beautiful grounds during the spring and summer months.

Craig and his classmates learned the stories behind each of the missions: how Father Serra ministered to the Native Americans in the area, establishing a standard of servanthood that later Catholic missionaries to the region sought to follow. Father Serra refused to ride on horseback unless it was absolutely necessary; he believed missionaries ought to walk and took this so seriously at one point he walked many miles on a wounded and bleeding leg. He took a vow of poverty and traveled without money or food, carrying only his breviary and relying on the kindness of people along the way for food and shelter.

Father Serra worked tirelessly to bring stability and prosperity to the Native American missions, providing cows, sheep, and goats to villagers and helping them learn how to expand and improve their agricultural efforts. He even advocated for Native Americans against the Spanish settlers, who at one point attempted to build a settlement on Native land. Father Serra appealed to the viceroy, arguing this was unjust. For years he pursued justice and eventually won the case; the Spanish settlers were relocated, and the Native Americans took back their land.

Craig and his classmates learned these stories and more from the life of Father Serra. They immersed themselves in the history of this good, just man, and learned about their own region in light of his life. They even made paper-mâché replicas of their favorite missions to present to their parents on back-to-school night.

Only a few years after Craig's tour of the missions, the narrative about Father Serra and the founding of the missions was completely flipped. By the time Craig was in middle school, a new and quite different story was being taught in California public schools.

This new history told impressionable fourth graders Father Serra and the Catholic fathers were evil oppressors who destroyed the Native American culture and tortured Native Americans into converting to Catholicism. While it is true several Native Americans experienced great cruelty in the colonial system of California, Father Serra stood up against that cruelty—at peril of his own safety and career—and denounced it as un-Christian.

Salvadore Joseph Cordileone, the archbishop of San Francisco, writes that Father Serra repeatedly intervened on behalf of indigenous rebels against secular Spanish authorities who were oppressing the Native Americans. At one point Serra walked on an excruciatingly painful ulcerated leg from California to Mexico City—quite a hike—to intercede for a Native tribe being abused. Archbishop Cordileone says, "If we looked at him with clear eyes, we would see Serra as one of the first American champions of the human rights of indigenous peoples."[11]

And until the 1970s, we had those clear eyes. This is the Father Serra students encountered in California public schools until Left-wing radicals managed to throw away this historical treasure.

Because of his association with traditional Christianity and evangelization, Father Junipero Serra has been vilified by those who wish to rewrite history, and his story is in danger of being entirely erased outside of Catholicism.

Statues of Father Serra have been removed in San Francisco and Los Angeles. In 2020, vandals tore down another statue of him, this one in Sacramento's Capitol Park. A radical group is trying to remove a statue of him from the U.S. Capitol.

Bishop Jamie Soto of the Sacramento Catholic Diocese has been active in setting the record straight on Father Serra's legacy. He said, "[W]hile Father Serra worked under the colonial system, he denounced its evils and worked to protect the dignity of native peoples. His holiness as a missionary should not be measured by his own failures to stop the exploitation or even his own personal faults. Holiness, in the end, is more a result of God's grace and our willingness to cooperate with His mercy."[12]

Bishop Soto's statement cuts directly to the heart of the problem with trying to erase Father Serra from history because he does not meet some people's standard of "perfection." Only one person has ever been perfect; He is Jesus Christ. Even the best individuals with the best intentions cannot be perfect. That was the message Father Serra brought with him to California—not one of bigotry and oppression. But instead of extending grace and mercy, Left-wing radicals try to damn anyone who does not live up to their own rapidly changing standards, standards that at any other time in history would have been unimaginable.

No person—past, present, or future—can live up to the standards of the radical Left. That is why we witness the frequent "cancellation" of people who were previously praised; no one can maintain a perfectly "woke" attitude at all times because the values of "wokeness" are constantly changing. What was acceptable yesterday may be damning today.

But radicals refuse to acknowledge the impossibility of their own standards. Instead, they are constantly engaged in an ongoing revision of history. Just as George Orwell wrote in *1984*, "Every book has been rewritten, every picture repainted, every statue and street and building has been renamed, every date has been altered,"[13] today the woke among us are constantly changing our society to fit this ever-shifting narrative—and applying the narrative backward in an after-the-fact condemnation and erasure of the past.

Orwell's novel famously describes the "Ministry of Truth," whose mission is to rewrite the past. Usually, the Ministry demonizes historical figures to advance the regime's current agenda, but in the novel the Ministry recasts historical events several times, sometimes praising them, sometimes condemning them—and everyone simply accepts the current narrative, even if it blatantly contradicts yesterday's telling.

Orwell's prophetic warnings are starting to become reality. In early 2020, Representative Alexandria Ocasio-Cortez proposed the government establish a truth initiative that did not agree with the current cultural orthodoxy.[14] While Orwell might have had the year wrong, he definitely nailed the threat—eventually only one version of "truth" would be allowed and anything that does not affirm that "truth" either must be rewritten or erased.

No surprise should be shown after the DHS secretary announced in an April 2022 congressional hearing the formation of the Disinformation Governance Board. The details and inferences of this new government agency resonates from the pages of *1984*.

All the rewriting, renaming, and altering of history comes at great cost—the loss of a common history and heritage. The toppling of Father Serra and others is just a sad down payment on a price far too high for us to pay: the loss of our heritage of mutual respect, freedom, and opportunity, grounded in the sacrifices of those who went before.

This is more of a loss than it may seem. Leon Kass, professor emeritus of the Committee on Social Thought at the University of Chicago, said in an interview with Anne Snyder for *Breaking Ground*, though English uses the words *nation* and *people* interchangeably, they mean very different things.

Kass said a "nation" is a group sharing a common ancestor (hence the Cherokee Nation, made up of people who share Cherokee blood). With this definition in place, it is clear Americans are not a nation—we do not share a common ethnic or familial ancestor. But, at least in the past, we have been a "people," which Kass says is "defined in terms of a common history, common mores, common songs, stories, culture, a common way of life, common aspirations,"[15] rather than common ancestry. Strip us of this common history and culture, and we have nothing left.

Jarrett Stepman writes in his book *The War on History*, "There is a spreading belief that the men who built this country were oppressive and their values irredeemable. The purveyors of this view argue that we must transcend the ugly ideas, principles, and even people of the past to perfect our society. We must transform America by wiping out previous generations celebrated as exceptional, but we know to be damnable."[16]

Yet, it was those previous generations who created what, over time, became the freest country on earth. Those generations fought for the end of slavery, brought an end to human genocide of the Nazis, and guaranteed religious freedom for all. But now, because of the "new" standards, nothing they did is acceptable in the eyes of the "woke."

Historian Harold Holzer, director of Hunter College's Roosevelt House of Public Policy Institute, says, "there's a danger in applying 21st-century moral standards to historical figures of one or two centuries ago. We expect everyone to be perfect. We expect everyone to be enlightened. But an enlightened person of 1865 is not the same as an enlightened person of 2021."[17] If we hold people from history to our own contemporary standards, we gain nothing, but we lose access to a vast store of wisdom and experience.

In July 2020, George Washington University announced it established committees to consider requests for the school's nickname, "the Colonials," to be retired. This nickname was meant to honor George Washington, but it has come under fire as "glorifying colonialism," which is defined as a system allowing white men to possess slaves. Some George Washington University students feel Washington is a "negatively charged figure" with "too deep a connection to colonization," and honoring him "glorifies the act of systemic oppression."[18]

On June 15, 2022, the committee announced, in accordance with the school's board of trustees, the "Colonials" nickname, in their words, "can no longer serve its purpose as a name that unifies." They went on to say the committee "found that the Colonials moniker does not adequately match values of GW," and when the name was first adapted in 1926, those who selected it lacked "thoughtful university-wide consideration." The committee then added, "Colonials mean colonizers who stole land and resources from indigenous groups, killed or exiled Native peoples and introduced slavery into the colonies"; a moniker must "unify our community, draw people together, and serve as a source of pride," and they looked forward to "the next steps in an inclusive process to identify a moniker that fulfills this aspiration."[19]

There is so much here that is off-base it is hard to know where to start. But first of all, I doubt those who chose the name in 1926 sat around the table and thought about the possible "thoughtlessness" of their nickname selection. In 1926, George Washington and the colonists who fought for our freedom were heroes to be honored—and respect for the sacrifice they made unified instead of divided our country. It has only been after the Leftist takeover of our educational system that our national heroes—who are now expected to be in tune with "woke" theology of 2022 or be cancelled—are seen as villains.

Second, actions such as this, for a relatively innocent moniker like the "Colonials," further divide our country, rather than unify it. For the left, unity means you have to absolutely agree with them. No disagreement is possible. That is totalitarianism, which is on full display with this action by the special committee and Board of Trustees at George Washington University.

Washington is not the only figure being targeted. Activists at the school also filed requests to rename campus buildings named after James Madison, James Monroe, Francis Scott Key, Senator William Fulbright, and Winston Churchill.

As one student said, some historical figures "don't deserve to be on campus anymore."[20]

Washington has also come under attack at the University of Washington in Seattle where a student group is demanding his statue be removed.[21] In Chicago, Mayor Lori Lightfoot said forty-one monuments, including monuments of Washington and Abraham Lincoln, would be "reconsidered" as part of a "historical reckoning project."[22] Before you know it, the bulldozers will be showing up at Lincoln's home in Springfield and at Washington's estate at Mt. Vernon.

Fortunately, some parents and community members (even in the Leftist haven of San Francisco) have voiced their belief that this laser-focus on destroying our history has gone too far—especially when it distracts administrators from providing a quality education.

In the middle of the COVID-19 pandemic in 2020, when schools were closed and teachers, parents, and students struggled to adjust to the immense pressure of online learning, the San Francisco Board of Education decided their first priority was not finding ways to support children but renaming schools named after America's founders. While the schools sat empty and students, parents, and teachers alike crumbled under a massive weight of anxiety and depression, school board members sat around voting to remove "Washington," "Lincoln," and other famous Americans' names from schools.

Grant Addison, a reporter at the *Washington Examiner*, found their decision-making had nothing to do with trying to provide an accurate study of history for students. Rather, he found the school board used Wikipedia in deciding which names to keep and which to abandon—even though teachers routinely warn students not to use Wikipedia as a source because the information it gives is so often incorrect (to put it mildly).

Addison recounts that during the meeting, a committee member used Wikipedia to claim nineteenth-century poet and diplomat James Russell Lowell did not want "black people to vote." Addison corrects the record, quoting instead a recent scholarly biography of Lowell that found Lowell advocated for giving recently freed slaves the right to vote.

Addison concludes,

> One might think that consulting a historian would have been beneficial to this process. Yet committee chairman Jeremiah Jeffries openly scoffed at the idea. "What would be the point? History is written and documented pretty well across the board. . . . Based on our criteria, it's a very straightforward conversation. And so, no need to bring historians forward to say—they either pontificate and list a bunch of reasons why, or [say] they had great qualities. Neither are necessary in this discussion." Much of history is indeed documented "pretty well across the board," yet that didn't stop these pompous cretins from getting easily verifiable facts wrong.[23]

Upon learning this expunging of history, not providing support for students and teachers, was the school board's priority, one parent said, "This is a bit of a joke. It's almost like a parody of leftist activism."[24]

After a parental outcry, the school board paused its plan, at least until the COVID-19 pandemic came to an end.[25]

Another example of something that seems like a joke but isn't, the new curriculum unanimously approved by the

California Department of Education for its schools, a curriculum so horrific both conservatives and reasoned liberals are opposed to it. The *Wall Street Journal* editorialized it would teach children the American creed was "sinister."[26] Even the highly liberal *Los Angeles Times* condemned the first draft of the curriculum as an "impenetrable mélange of academic jargon and politically correct pronouncements."[27]

Under the guise of "ethnic studies," the curriculum requires students to chant to the Aztec god of human sacrifice and cannibalism[28] and accuses white Christians (such as Father Serra) of committing "theocide" against indigenous peoples and murdering their "gods" as the first step toward "coloniality, dehumanization, and genocide." Students are then forced to engage in "countergenocide" and "counterhegemony," so the "regeneration of indigenous epistemic and cultural futurity" can be achieved.[29]

Basically, the state of California has declared war on Western civilization and is brainwashing students as young as kindergarten to be its soldiers.

The curriculum is selective about whose experience counts as "victimhood" (a quality excusing all past and future sins). Bret Stephens called out the curriculum's double standard in the *New York Times* (of all places), writing, "'Ethnic studies is for all students,' the curriculum announces. Actually, not so much. Irish Americans have faced a long history of discrimination in the U.S. and are famously proud of their heritage. But the word 'Irish' hardly appears anywhere in the model curriculum, and nowhere in its sample lessons. Russians, Italians, Poles, and others rate only the briefest mentions."[30]

He continues, "Ethnic studies is less an academic discipline than it is the recruiting arm of a radical ideological movement masquerading as mainstream pedagogy. From the opening pages of the model curriculum, students are expected not just to 'challenge racist, bigoted, discriminatory, imperialist/colonial beliefs,' but to 'critique empire-building in history' and 'connect ourselves to past and contemporary social movements that struggle for social justice.'"[31]

It is telling that those who wish to radically change our society do not advocate for improved, deepened, or broadened history curricula. They do not advocate for a more thorough telling of America's story; one considering the experience of groups as diverse as Chippewa, Irish, Ojibwe, Russian, Senegambian, Mexican, Spanish, and the countless others who have met and mingled in this land; one that includes our founders' faults and hopes side-by-side and situates them and their aspirations within a balanced historical context.

They would probably find a great deal of enthusiasm for this project across the political spectrum. Many conservatives would also appreciate a deeper historical look at America's founding, one that does not gloss over atrocities like the egregious treaty that drove the Cherokee from their ancestral lands in Georgia but instead tells those stories alongside stories of goodness, virtue, and partnership between Europeans and other groups, including indigenous peoples.

But today's radical activists are not interested in improving our collective understanding of our past. They are not interested in a deeper knowledge of where we as a people come from. They are only interested in erasing our past, bulldozing our heritage, and demolishing our culture, so they can set up a new one—one with no ties to "life, liberty, and the pursuit of happiness" and no homage to God-given rights.

## THE SIN OF SLAVERY

It is impossible to talk about American history without talking about slavery and the slave trade. Slavery was, and is, abhorrent. It should not be glamorized, affirmed, or justified in any form. It is also part of the human story and an unavoidable part of the American story. As such, we must do our best to understand what role slavery played in early America and how that role changed over time.

In the early years of America, the sin of slavery was widespread in Europe (as well as around the world in Africa, China, central Asia, and among Native America tribes such as the Pawnee and the Yurok).[32] Most English people of means owned slaves or directly benefited from slavery.

This was perceived as socially acceptable, though by the mid-nineteenth century this perception was changing. In Jane Austen's *Mansfield Park*, published in 1814, we see the abolition movement in England just beginning to penetrate mainstream thought. But in the sixteenth and seventeenth centuries, the main moral objections to slavery were rooted in how slaves were treated, not in the fact they were slaves. In this environment, social morality demanded not that everyone free their slaves, but that they treat their slaves kindly.

Clearly, from our vantage point in the twenty-first century, we can see the insufficiency of this demand. But in trying to understand those who came before us, we must see how they measure up to the moral standards of *their day*. We must also measure people equally, not assigning blame to historical figures to further a narrative.

Here is an example of an undeniable fact: George Washington owned slaves. So did Thomas Jefferson. That is a historical fact. We need not affirm their decisions to own slaves and, in fact, can be critical about it, but we must understand that decision in its historical and social context, and we must not condemn all of Washington's and Jefferson's decisions and actions because we have learned, as a society, this one was not acceptable.

If this sounds like I am making excuses to protect a historical character of two of our Founding Fathers, let me offer a second example to illustrate:

Chief Seattle was a nineteenth-century Suquamish and Duwamish chief in the Pacific Northwest. The city of Seattle was named after him. Throughout his long, adventurous life, Chief Seattle fought tirelessly and creatively—using military force, economic intelligence, and social and cultural awareness—to preserve his people's heritage and land. He commanded the respect of friend and foe alike, earning accolades from enemy tribes and from European settlers who were often thwarted by his efforts. He labored to preserve his tribes' land rights, as well as their cultural respect for the environment, in a time of rapid agricultural expansion and settlement on the Puget Sound. He left a legacy of immense value to all Americans to this day.

He also, for a period of his life, owned slaves.

Should we reject Chief Seattle's insights into humanity's relationship with the environment because he held slaves for a while? Should we ignore his call to respect the land and rights of Native Americans? Should we rename the city of Seattle and tear down his statues because one element of his storied life does not align with our twenty-first-century understanding of morality?

The answer here is obvious. The story of Chief Seattle deserves to be *more* widely told, not less—his words better known and his legacy more clearly understood. Yes, he held slaves; we must not ignore that. But he was more than a slaveholder.

That is the difficult thing about history: no one is reducible to a single biographical fact. Chief Seattle was a slaveholder. He was also a champion for the environment. George Washington was a slaveholder. Thomas Jefferson was a slaveholder. They also fought for the rights of working-class Americans to not be taxed unfairly by the English monarchy.

As we read history and learn about history figures, we must look at their whole lives, the broad range of their actions and decisions, and evaluate them through as many factors as we can, rather than reducing them to one fact or characteristic.

Washington, Jefferson, and many of the other founders who held slaves showed in their writings that they hoped slavery would one day end. In his will, Washington asked his slaves to be freed. In fact, late in life, he expressed deep regret over owning slaves,[33] as would Jefferson, which I will discuss in a bit. They did not do the difficult work of ending it themselves, and for that our nation continues to suffer to this day. But through their writings and the values they established, they laid the foundation that would eventually bring the abhorrent practice to an end.

Glenn Loury is a Black professor at Brown University who also serves as president of the Manhattan Institute. He wrote about this very issue, saying of the ending of slavery in America,

> It shouldn't have taken 100 years; they shouldn't
> have been slaves in the first place. True enough. But
> slavery had been a commonplace human experience
> since antiquity. Emancipation—the freeing of slaves

en masse, the movement for abolition—that was a
new idea. A Western idea. The fruit of Enlighten-
ment. An idea that was brought to fruition over a
century and a half ago here, in the United States of
America, liberating millions of people and creating
the world we now inhabit.

This great and historic achievement surely
would not have been possible without philosophical
insights and moral commitments cultivated in the
seventeenth and eighteenth centuries in the West—
ideas about the essential dignity of human persons
and about what makes a government's exercise of
power over its people legitimate. But something
new was created here in America at the end of the
eighteenth century. Slavery was a holocaust out of
which emerged something that actually advanced
the morality and the dignity of humankind—namely,
emancipation. The abolition of slavery and the
incorporation of Africa-descended people into the
body politic of the United States of America was an
unprecedented achievement.[34]

The struggles Washington and Jefferson expressed over
the issue of slavery, the fact it was debated at all during the
founding of our nation and there were strong voices for its
abolition, coupled with the principles—albeit, acted upon
slower than they probably should have—embedded in America's founding documents, make it clear many of our founders
struggled mightily with their conscience on this issue.

That is why interpretating history is not an easy discipline.
It does not allow us to settle into easy dichotomies or straightforward praise and blame. Every event and every person is a

complicated mix of actions, decisions, and impulses playing out in a certain culture and society.

History is the record of those events and those people. It is not a clear-cut, good-versus-evil story; it is a vast, complex account of what has come before us. It helps us understand why we are the way we are now, and it helps us learn from the past—both the good and the bad. Erasing either that which is praiseworthy or that which is blameworthy leaves us adrift, unsure of how to orient ourselves and move forward toward greater virtue.

Therefore, we build monuments and raise statues to remember. Not every monument is aggrandizing. The monuments scattered across Eastern Europe dedicated to victims of the Holocaust serve to remind us of the evil humanity is capable of and the incalculable value of every individual life.

As Kay James, a Black American and the former president of The Heritage Foundation wrote, "We have built statues and memorials to recognize individuals and events representing some of the noblest—and even some of the worst—moments in our history. The people memorialized didn't lead perfect lives, and many did controversial or even evil things, but monuments help tell our history and help us remember our highest ideals—as well as the mistakes we've made and wish not to repeat again."[35]

For instance, the late civil rights champion Congressman John Lewis said about Thomas Jefferson, "We knew about Jefferson's faults, but we didn't put the emphasis there. We put the emphasis on what he wrote in the Declaration . . . . His words were so powerful. His words became the blueprint, the guideline for us to follow."[36]

We must commend men like Washington and Jefferson for what they did right—providing the framework that created the freest nation on earth—while not dismissing their faults. It is a matter of emphasis. The radical progressive attitude toward American history elevates the faults while burying the virtues. This attitude wants to erase any memory of our flawed foundations from our collective memory—even if that leaves us completely homeless, disoriented, and ungrateful.

This is the attitude of the small but persistent group of radicals who compelled the mayor of Charlottesville, Virginia, famously the home of Thomas Jefferson, to replace Jefferson's birthday with "Liberation and Freedom Day."[37] This is the attitude of University of Virginia students who gathered to protest their school's founder and "white supremacy," placing placards on his statue calling him a "racist" and "rapist."[38] This is the attitude of those who call for an end to public funding for the Jefferson Memorial in Washington, DC, and the removal of Jefferson's statue to a private museum.[39]

As Jarrett Stepman wrote in his book *The War on History*, "This is a shabby way to treat the legacy of a man who contributed, in so many ways, great and small, to who we are today."[40]

Congressman John Lewis recognized what these radical activists have not. Jefferson was a slaveowner who allegedly had a mistress who bore his children (though not conclusively proven). But he was also the author of the Declaration of Independence, a visionary document John Lewis called "the blueprint" to freedom[41] and Martin Luther King described as a "promissory note—a promise that all men would be guaranteed the inalienable rights of life, liberty, and the pursuit of happiness."[42]

Yes, Jefferson was far from perfect. We are all far from perfect. History is not the study of perfect people but of profound people, influential people, people with ideas and actions that made the rest of the world sit up and take notice. Christians should have no problem with acknowledging the failures of historical figures; the Bible is full of men and women who, despite their flaws, served God and showed us God's truth.

As we bring the Bible to the discussion, I have an observation about what foments the Left's rabid destruction of American history: unforgiveness and ingratitude. In discarding the authority of God and His standards, with that goes the core of the gospel. Christ died to open the gates of forgiveness for our sin and whether the Left wants to acknowledge the truth or not, *all* have sinned. That includes every statue and name remover on college campuses.

Rather than abandoning our Founding Fathers because of their own failings, Americans should instead look at them in awe that such flawed men were able to have a pure vision and were able to take grave personal risks to achieve that vision. In large part, our Founding Fathers failed on the issue of slavery. Their personal failure is not the surprising part of the story. The surprise is, despite this failure, they envisioned and developed a system of government like nothing seen on earth up until that time: a system of government affirming human dignity and eventually leading to the end of slavery.

Carol Swain, retired professor of history at Vanderbilt University and vice-chairman of the 1776 Commission (which I will discuss later), said,

> Did I know, growing up, that George Washington and Thomas Jefferson owned slaves? I don't think I ever thought about it. If I did, I'd like to think that I would have had enough common sense to know that we can't judge men who lived 250 years ago by

the moral standards of our own day . . . . But I know that Jefferson wrote the words in the Declaration of Independence that made slavery ultimately impossible: that all men are created equal. And I know that Washington, Hamilton, Franklin, Adams and the rest of the Founders risked everything to make my world, my America, possible. How could I not be grateful for that and for the sacrifices so many others have made to preserve it?[43]

Historian James Byrd, chair of the Graduate Department of Religion and associate professor of American Religious History at Vanderbilt University Divinity School, writes in his book *A Holy Baptism of Fire and Blood* that Washington and Jefferson saw slavery as a necessary (to keep the South in the Union) evil and hoped one day soon Americans would end it. There were others among the early Americans, such as the Southerner John C. Calhoun and his supporters, who believed slavery was a "moral institution" and threw up numerous obstacles to make sure the existence of the Union depended on preserving slavery.[44] Whether men like Jefferson and Washington ought to have made this bargain for the sake of the nation is a fraught question: America would have been highly unlikely to succeed in its war for freedom without the South's support.

Looking at it from our vantage point of the future, it is easy to say they should have stood firm and refused to allow slavery in the new nation. Looking at it from within their present moment, as best we can, the question is more difficult—and provides better insights into our own day. How are good and evil tangled up in the justice movements of our own day? What broken systems are we propping up for the sake of other goods, like the founders did? What evils are so intrinsic to society and culture today that we cannot see them for what they are?

An obsession with the flaws of historical figures without an equal focus on their good contributions distorts our view of history—and of our own historical moment. Thanks to what is being taught in America's classrooms, many students now say America invented slavery and there is no historical record of it occurring anywhere else. In reality, African slaves were imported to America by foreign entities who also brought them to Brazil, the Caribbean, and the West Indies; and slavery has been a part of human history since before civilizations kept records.

One professor found in a poll of thirty-two of his students, twenty-nine knew Jefferson owned slaves, but only three knew Jefferson was a president.[45] And few people know that at the end of his life, Jefferson, like Washington, expressed his greatest regret was not being able to do away with the institution of slavery. He and his colleagues came incredibly close to eliminating slavery in the Commonwealth of Virginia in 1784. According to Jefferson, the bill failed by one vote. This failure haunted him to his dying day.

Despite this, Jefferson did play a pivotal role in the passage of the Northwest Ordinance under the Articles of Confederation, a law barring slavery in the territory that eventually became the states of Ohio, Illinois, Indiana, Michigan, Minnesota, and Wisconsin. These states became the industrial backbone of the Union during the Civil War and sacrificed tens of thousands of men to the cause of freedom.

Finally, few people know Jefferson, like Washington, attempted to free his own slaves. He did not manage to do so because the laws of his time made it almost impossible to ensure they would remain free and not fall into the hands of a less benevolent owner. For Jefferson, situated as he was in a society that permitted slavery, it seemed like the most morally sound choice to keep his slaves, so they would not suffer under a cruel master. Was this choice right or wrong? That would be an excellent question for a robust, fact-based history curriculum to pose to thoughtful students grounded in a strong sense of what Jefferson's society was really like, as well as an awareness that some goods—like the good of individual freedom—are not historically relative.

Before any teacher posed this question, however, she would have to let Jefferson plead his cause in his own words. A year before he died, Jefferson wrote,

> At the age of 82, with one foot in the grave and the other uplifted to follow it, I do not permit myself to take part in any new enterprises . . . not even the great one [the emancipation of slaves] which has been through life that one of my greatest anxieties. The march of events has not been such as to render its completion practicable within the limits of time allotted to me . . . . The abolishment of this evil is not impossible; it ought never therefore to be despaired of. Every plan should be adopted, every experiment tried, which may do something towards the ultimate object.[46]

These do not sound like the words of a cruel oppressor but, rather, of a dying man reflecting on his own failures and regrets. This is the nature of history—of the human experience, in fact: No one is perfect. No life (except Christ's) is flawless. No good is unmitigated.

History helps us learn the truth of what happened before we were born, and inevitably that truth is complex and messy. When we teach the life of Thomas Jefferson, those lessons must reflect that. We should not teach him as a perfect person, but neither should we teach him as purely evil. The truth is (as it usually is) far more interesting than either of those extremes.

When we approach Thomas Jefferson as a human being who can teach us, both from his failures and from his successes, we find a brilliant writer, a daring rebel for the cause of liberty, a political visionary, a slaveowner tangled in the social evil of his day—all side by side. We cannot eliminate any of these elements. But here in some of his final words we see his regrets that he could not do more to ensure the freedom of all Americans—regardless of race, color, or creed. This is a historical insight as much as a personal one, and it shows us what motivated Jefferson in his successes and embittered his failings.

As Jarrett Stepman writes, "It is easy to condemn Jefferson and the Founders for not doing enough to extinguish a social system now universally reviled . . . . Slavery was woven into the cultural and economic fabric of American society, and it could not be easily removed even by those who deeply hated it. Given this reality, it is perhaps less remarkable that they failed immediately to rid themselves of it, and more remarkable that their efforts put it on the inevitable path to extinction."[47]

The radicals who have taken over our nation's educational system are not interested in history, in the difficult questions it poses about good, evil, justice, and equality. They are not seeking an accurate and balanced treatment of our nation's founders. They are not interested in grounding young people in a historical awareness that helps them understand their own time and place and make moral decisions about how to live. Rather, they are interested in brainwashing, in moral stagnation, in crushing young people's critical thinking, so they are unable to make their own decisions and rely instead on instructions from above.

All of this works together to teach students our whole system of government, with its balance of power between three branches and its careful representation of all people in all regions of our nation, is corrupt and unredeemable.

This may be the first time in history a nation has used its tax dollars to teach its young citizens the nation is utterly corrupt. That is our absurd situation: our government is funding lessons and textbooks insisting our governmental system is evil!

To make these claims, radicals must suppress a huge portion of history—namely, anything indicating America and our innovative system of government has been a force of good in the world—as we will see in our next chapter when I discuss the work of Howard Zinn and other "revisionist" historians.

This is one arm of the leviathan known as "cancel culture," reaching into history textbooks across America to remove and bury all the people and facts that go against the progressive narrative. Its victims include not only Washington and Jefferson but also Franklin Roosevelt, Theodore Roosevelt, Charles Dickens, Winston Churchill, and numerous others.[48]

This divisive, damaging practice may have one unintended good consequence: conservatives and liberals from across the political spectrum have joined to denounce cancel culture in the classroom.

Bari Weiss, a self-described liberal and a former opinion writer for *The New York Times*, resigned after seeing how cancel culture played out in her newsroom. She writes frequently about the dangers of subjugating history to wokeness. In an article for *Deseret News* in March 2021, Weiss wrote of cancel culture, "The primary mode of this ideological movement is not building or renewing or reforming but tearing down. Persuasion is replaced with public shaming. Forgiveness is replaced with punishment. Mercy is replaced with vengeance. Pluralism with conformity; debate with de-platforming; facts with feelings; ideas with identity."[49]

Weiss agrees with others that the result of this new "illiberalism," as she calls it, is the past can no longer be understood on its own terms. Instead, the morals and mores of the present must be applied to it. She writes, "Education, according to this ideology, is not about teaching people how to think, it's about telling them what to think."[50]

She shares many examples, but one stands out: William Peris, an Air Force veteran and a lecturer in political science at UCLA, triggered a U.S. Department of Education investigation after he read Martin Luther King's "Letter from Birmingham Jail" out loud. The text of King's letter includes the n-word. Peris also played a documentary clip containing a graphic image of a lynching.[51]

This content is understandably distressing, but the course was about the history of racism in the United States. No treatment of this subject can avoid being distressing. By trying to punish Peris for reading King's own words and for showing what was actually happening in American history, the Department of Education is working *against* exposing the full truth of racial injustice in America. Suppressing this truth and requiring us as a people to "forget" it could have the disastrous consequence of forcing us to relive it.

Such cancellations, such distorted historical narratives, such rejections of the basic truths our country was founded on—all these things have a way of spilling out of the classroom and into our lives. Weiss writes that when she was growing up, in the 1980s, Americans shared a "consensus view": "[T]he belief that everyone is created in the image of God; the belief that everyone is equal because of it; the presumption of innocence; a revulsion to mob justice; a commitment to pluralism and free speech, and to liberty of thought and of faith."

This view spanned the political spectrum. In fact, it transcended it; because people from all classes, all races, all faiths, and all political creeds shared these basic convictions, Americans who disagreed on almost everything else could share a life and a society. Neighbors of differing political convictions could sit together at a cookout without secretly (or not so secretly) believing the other to be a monster. They could sit next to each other in the church pew and worship God. Families of differing faiths or with different ideas about was is good could be in a room together. As Weiss puts it, the American consensus "recognized that there were whole realms of human life located outside the province of politics, like friendships, art, music, family and love."

This consensus is not just a way to make society more pleasant. It is the whole foundation of America. It is the only thing holding us together. Americans do not share blood ties; we do not share a single creed; we do not even live in similar places or climates because of the vastness of our country. All we have is, as Weiss puts it, "a commitment to a shared set of ideas." And for more than two hundred years, that was enough.

This, Weiss says, is what makes America truly exceptional, what sets us apart from every existent nation up until 1776: "[America] is a departure from the notion, still prevalent in so many other places, that biology, birthplace, class, rank, gender, race are destiny. Our second Founding Fathers, abolitionists like Frederick Douglass, were living testimonies to that truth." This consensus of ideas—freedom of thought and expression is a basic human right; people can live together despite their different classes, races, and creeds; the image of God in each individual unifies us—is what radical progressives are trying to dismantle. In its place, they are setting up the kind of brutal, unforgiving tribalism pitting human against human since the beginning of time.

There is an obvious progressive response to this: the radical changes to history and society embodied in cancel culture are merely a kind of consensus. The strictures and prohibitions of cancel culture, progressives might say, are merely a kind of taboo, a feature of all functional societies.

Weiss addresses this response, pointing out taboos only work to bring about a healthy social unity when they arise naturally from the community. When they are imposed from above, they fracture the community. She writes, "[I]n the past, societal taboos were generally reached through a cultural consensus. Today's taboos, on the other hand, are often fringe ideas pushed by a zealous cabal trying to redefine what is acceptable and what should be shunned. It is a group that has control of nearly all the institutions that produce American cultural and intellectual life: media, to be sure, but also higher education, museums . . . [and] K-12 education."[52]

This top-down enforcement of artificial "taboos" has frightening precedents. Just look at the so-called cultural revolution in China in the late 1960s and early '70s, where

Mao Zedong brutally imposed a taboo on all Western influences. To restore what he claimed was "pure" Chinese culture, Zedong forbade anything from the West, particularly anything he decided was representative of "bourgeois." His Red Guards destroyed monuments, renamed buildings, and burned Western literature—and this was just the beginning.

Very quickly, the revolution escalated, and the Red Guards imprisoned, brutalized, and murdered anyone suspected of importing Western values. This could be as simple as being a teacher or being an intellectual who in the past studied the West. Churches in particular suffered under the cultural revolution; many were destroyed, and many pastors and religious leaders imprisoned. This culture of enforced conformity continues to haunt China today. Christian congregations are forced to worship in secret. Religious minorities, like the Uighur Muslims in the northwest of China, are being shipped to nightmarish concentration camps, brainwashed, tortured, and systematically exterminated.

This resulted from an attempt to impose a taboo from the top down. It started by destroying "corrupt" monuments, censoring unacceptable literature, and renaming buildings and mountains in national parks—all of which was already happening in America in 2021 and has been amplified since Joe Biden took the White House.

## RESEGREGATING AMERICA

In a piece for the *Wall Street Journal*, Andrew Michta writes about another way cancel culture shatters the unity of American culture. He writes how radicals have turned race "into a lens through which to view the country's history" in order to "identify and separate these groups that deserve affirmation, in their view, and those that do not." The result is the resegregation of America.[53]

Segregation was the social (and often legal) system establishing separate societies for Black and White Americans—and punished Black Americans who infringed on what were perceived to be "white" areas or privileges. The system perpetuated the injustices of slavery for more than a century after Lincoln signed the Emancipation Proclamation, keeping Black Americans from the rights and responsibilities justly theirs as citizens of our country. The civil rights movement of the 1950s and 1960s was focused on ending segregation in all its forms and giving Blacks and other minorities access to the same opportunities to flourish as White Americans.

Segregation was an aberration from the American ideal; in other words, it was quite simply a violation of the principles laid out by Jefferson and the signers of the Declaration of Independence. When our founders wrote that all men had unalienable rights including the right to life, liberty, and the pursuit of happiness, they set in motion a political system defending all human beings' equal access to the rights and privileges that come with being human. Segregation spurned that vision.

That is why civil rights heroes like Martin Luther King Jr., T. R. M. Howard, Rosa Parks, and Jo Ann Gibson Robinson are seen as American heroes: these individuals saw American failing to meet its own standards and pushed our country to reject injustice and strive for the equality written into our founding documents.

But now, as radicals are tearing apart the principles undergirding equality and justice—and just as you would expect, leading to a new form of the segregation the civil rights movement fought to overcome—and as children and university students are being taught that rather than living together in unity, we must instead focus on the perceived grievances we have against each other.

There is another way forward. Instead of tearing down statues, destroying legacies, erasing memories, and dividing our nation, there is a way to move forward in unity. Instead of wiping out the past, we can look at it even more closely and learn from it. The past can divide us, but it can also reconcile us.

Consider, for example, the historical figure of Frederick Douglass. This hero of American history has received far too little attention for his role in bringing reconciliation while also calling out sin.

Frederick Douglass was born in 1818 to a female Black slave and an unidentified White father in Talbot County, Maryland. As was common at the time, he and his mother were separated when he was quite young, and he lived with his grandparents until the age of six. For the first two decades of his life, he was treated like a piece of property, bought and sold by various masters. One of his master's wives taught him the alphabet, though her husband later convinced her slaves should not be literate.

Douglass, however, turned these scanty lessons to his advantage, and secretly over the years he taught himself to read and write. This enabled him to learn more about slavery from books and other publications, and Douglass began to envision a free life for himself. Upon being traded to a master in Baltimore, Douglass met and fell in love with a free Black woman named Anna Murray, who encouraged him to seek freedom. Eventually Douglass escaped to New York, a free state, and sent for Murray to join him. They married in New York.

It was in New York where Douglass became a frequent speaker at antislavery meetings. His fervent, learned speeches inspired many to join the antislavery cause. He went on to write and publish the account of his successful escape from slavery, titled *Narrative of the Life of Frederick Douglass.* The book became a best seller—a mixed blessing, as his newfound notoriety put him in danger of being captured and returned to his former owner.

But Douglass would not be deterred from telling the truth about slavery. He traveled to Great Britain and Ireland, testifying about the brutality and inhumanity of the slave system, and was able to raise enough money to purchase his release from slavery.

Douglass returned to New York, where he advocated alongside suffragette Elizabeth Cady Stanton for women's right to vote, sheltered slaves escaping from the South, and led the battle to stop racial segregation in public schools.

Douglass went on to serve as an advisor on race issues to two presidents: Abraham Lincoln and Ulysses S. Grant. During the Civil War, Douglass served as a recruiter for the first Black army regiment. Two of his sons joined that regiment. In meetings with Lincoln, Douglass pushed for equal pay and treatment for Black soldiers and advised the president on how to best help escaped slaves. When President Grant sent federal troops into the Carolinas to disrupt the activities of the Ku Klux Klan, Douglass applauded his efforts and rallied support for the president among Black and White Americans alike.

Frederick Douglass was a brilliant, gifted writer and speaker, but more than that, he was a principled, perceptive man who mastered the difficult art of blaming evil while praising good, and not ignoring either. There are few better examples of this art than in his keynote address delivered at the dedication of the Emancipation Memorial in 1876.

In this speech, Douglass did not veil his frustrations and criticisms of President Lincoln. He said, "[Lincoln] was ready and willing at any time during the first years of his administration to deny, postpone, and sacrifice the rights of humanity in the colored people to promote the welfare of the white people of this country." He rightly pointed out Lincoln was, for several years, willing to postpone the emancipation of the slaves indefinitely if this postponement would prevent civil war.

Lincoln, Douglass said, was primarily interested in two things: "first, to save his country from dismemberment and ruin; and, second, to free his country from the great crime of slavery." To accomplish the first, Douglass says, Lincoln was willing to forestall the second—until it became clear that the South would not tolerate any limitations on slavery and was determined to carry slavery into the new American territories.

Douglass does not try to hide his frustration with Lincoln's delays on emancipation. But he also does not condemn Lincoln. Rather, he recognizes the impossible situation Lincoln found himself in: if he freed the slaves, he risked losing the Union, and if he lost the Union, he would be unable to enforce the laws freeing the slaves. As Douglass said, "Had he put the abolition of slavery before the salvation of the Union, he would have inevitably driven from him a powerful class of the American people and rendered resistance to rebellion impossible. Viewed from the genuine abolition ground, Mr. Lincoln seemed tardy, cold, dull, and indifferent; but measuring him by the sentiment of his country, a sentiment he was bound as a statesman to consult, he was swift, zealous, radical, and determined."

These two sentences are a masterclass in historical analysis. Douglass models for us how we ought to measure the men and women of the past, not merely by our responses to their actions but by the sentiment and pressure of their cultures and societies—sentiments and pressures inevitably guiding their decisions. Douglass acknowledges Lincoln's actions were too slow for the ardent idealists among us, but considering the situation he was in (president of the United States), those actions were "swift, zealous, radical, and determined."

Douglass was speaking only fifteen years after the Civil War began. Even in that brief time, the gap between Lincoln's actions and the ideal was huge, and Douglass strove to help his audience bridge that gap. Now, after a hundred and fifty years, Douglass's words and his techniques are vastly more important—and almost impossible to find in today's historians.

Douglass summarized his attitude and that of other Black leaders in America toward Lincoln: a painful mingling of hope and disappointment, trust and dismay, respect and frustration. He said,

> The name of Abraham Lincoln was near and
> dear to our hearts in the darkest and most perilous
> hours of the Republic . . . . We saw him, measured
> him, and estimated him; not by stray utterances
> to injudicious and tedious delegations, who often
> tried his patience; not by isolated facts torn from
> their connection; not by any partial and imperfect
> glimpses, caught an inopportune moments; but by
> a broad survey, in the light of stern logic of great
> events, and in view of that divinity which shapes our
> ends, rough hew them how we will, we come to the

conclusion that the hour and man of our redemption had somehow met in the person of Abraham Lincoln.[54]

Douglass's words give us a razor-sharp image of Lincoln as a flawed but determined figure. But he gives us even more. He also gives us a method for viewing history—a way to exist in a world where nothing and no one is perfect, and where even those who we respect will frustrate and disappoint us. Douglass determines virtue not merely from isolated words and deeds but instead "by a broad survey, in the light of stern logic of great events, and in view of that divinity which shapes our ends." This kind of survey allows our heroes to be flawed; it expects them to stumble, and does not shoot them down when they do, but instead it holds them to the standard of "that divinity which shapes our ends," the perfection we only experience in God.

Currently, Douglass only has one national monument: a statue in the Emancipation Hall in the U.S. Capitol Visitors Center.[55] That is, quite simply, wrong. Douglass ought to be recognized as the major American figure he was: a complex, brilliant man who stood near the center of vast historical events and spoke boldly and clearly about how to interpret and respond to these events.

During the tumultuous summer of 2020, when mobs were tearing down statues across America, someone vandalized and destroyed a statue of Frederick Douglass standing in the city of Rochester, New York.[56] The statue was a well-known fixture of Rochester's Maplewood Rose Garden, which marks one of the ends of the famous Underground Railroad and the spot where many slaves fleeing along the route took their first free breath. On the night of July 5, 2020, the statue of Douglass was torn from its base and dragged to a nearby river, where it was abandoned.

This contemptible act of vandalism illustrates a grim truth: the tearing down of statues can go both ways. It is dangerous to approach history in a spirit of destruction because the tide of that destruction can quickly change. The study of history can never be about tearing down, about mandating forgetfulness and destroying the truth. It must always be about building up, about deepening and broadening our awareness of what happened before and what forces worked to bring us to our current moment.

Interestingly, there is a statue of Frederick Douglass on the grounds of Hillsdale College, a small conservative college in Michigan that has a long history of championing truth no matter the social costs. Douglass's statue stands alongside a statute commemorating the five hundred Hillsdale college students who volunteered to fight for the Union in the Michigan and Indiana infantry regiments in the Civil War. Hillsdale is a famously conservative college, one that continues to this day to teach from a strong Judeo-Christian heritage and to shape its students with a sense of patriotic duty toward their country. Hillsdale is also one of the few places in America that can boast a statue of Frederick Douglass. I will discuss this curious detail later in the context of the 1776 Commission, as it may point a way forward out of the morass of partisan historical bickering toward a truly unified and truly conservative vision of our nation.

Unity, unfortunately, is emphatically *not* what progressive radicals are proposing. Rather than uniting people around a deep, honest exploration of our shared past—the good and the bad—the new history curricula are an exercise in self-righteous finger-pointing at anyone who does not live up to contemporary standards of morality. This means vilifying and erasing even against those who stood for civil rights such as Abraham Lincoln, Ulysses S. Grant, and Theodore Roosevelt.

This is not what Reverend King had in mind in his famous "I Have a Dream" speech, nor is it the kind of careful observation and judgment for which Frederick Douglass advocated. Instead of the vision of Douglass for historical clarity and the dream of King for racial unity, progressives are dragging America into a dark and divided nightmare.

## 1619...

This brings me to the "1619 Project," promoted by the *New York Times* and named after the year the first Black slaves supposedly arrived in Jamestown. This project is an attempt to radically rewrite American history and advance the narrative that America was first and foremost—and continues to be— an oppressive slave state motivated and sustained by racism.

One of the presuppositions of the 1619 Project is the War for Independence was not fought to escape British tyranny but instead to preserve slavery.[57] The 1619 Project is the Trojan Horse, disguised under "academic inquiry," to indoctrinate an entire generation to radically change America.

In its feature on the 1619 Project, the *Times* wrote its intent was to show "our democracy's founding ideals were false when they were written."[58]

The problem is this: The author of the 1619 Project, Nikole Hannah-Jones, who won a Pulitzer Prize for it, freely admits the project has nothing to do with history. The presupposition of the project—the Founding Fathers were willfully deceptive about their motives for the Revolutionary War—flies in the face of the Founding Fathers' actual accounts. This, matched with the utter lack of evidence for the presupposition, should have made the project unviable. But Hannah-Jones neatly sidestepped the problem of history by saying, "I've always said the 1619 Project is not a history. It is a work of journalism that explicitly seeks to challenge the national narrative, and therefore, the national memory. The project has always been as much about the present as it is the past."[59]

What Hannah-Jones is doing with the 1619 Project is, in other words, a reading of the past through the lens of the present. It is not an attempt to better understand a complex, challenging moment in history by digging into the vast trove of historical evidence we have. Rather, Hannah-Jones discards historical evidence in favor of contemporary feelings. And, despite her assertion the project is not "a history," that is how it has been portrayed: as the true history of America. In its leading story on the project, the *New York Times* said the project "aims to reframe the country's history."[60] When this is the opening salvo, later claims by its advocates that the 1619 Project is not a history ring false.

The assertion the 1619 Project is not a historical project, but a journalistic one, allowed Hannah-Jones to sidestep the baseline requirements of historical research: evidence and accuracy. This is a neat loophole: Hannah-Jones was able to savage America's founding, gut America's ideals and principles, and accuse our founders of running a deep con by cloaking their desire to preserve the slave trade in the robes of a War of Independence; but when critics question the blatant inaccuracies and gaps in her research, she merely has to say her project was not intended to be "historical" but "journalistic."

And there are plenty of inaccuracies to criticize in the 1619 Project. For instance, the central premise of the project, in Hannah-Jones's own words, is this: "Conveniently left out of our founding mythology is the fact that one of the primary reasons the colonists decided to declare their independence from Britain was because they wanted to protect the institution of slavery."[61]

This is so blatantly false a historian who helped fact-check the 1619 Project for the *New York Times* raised concerns before the project was even published. The *Times* reached out to Dr. Leslie Harris, a historian at Northwestern University who specializes in Black life and slavery in the pre-Civil War era, for input on the exact claim quoted above. Harris explained, Hannah-Jones's claim was completely untrue. So, she was shocked when the *Times* ignored her and ran Hannah-Jones's claim with no caveats or corrections. Harris wrote in an article for *Politico*, published seven months after the release of the 1619 Project, "I vigorously disputed the claim. Although slavery was certainly an issue in the American Revolution, the protection of slavery was not one of the main reasons the 13 Colonies went to war."[62]

Dr. Harris holds a PhD from Stanford University in American history. She teaches and publishes regularly on pre-Civil War Black labor history and the history of slavery in the United States. She is a recognized expert in this field. But the *New York Times* and Nikole Hannah-Jones completely ignored her input and published the false claim in the finished project—facts can be sticky if they get in the way of advancing a narrative.

When Dr. Harris published her piece in *Politico*, Hannah-Jones finally tweaked the false claim—seven months after the original publication. Dr. Harris's essay pointed out other errors in the 1619 Project, specifically, "[T]he paper's characterizations of slavery in early America reflected laws and practices more common in the antebellum era than in Colonial times and did not accurately illustrate the varied experiences of the first generation of enslaved people that arrived in Virginia in 1619."[63]

As of this book's publication, Hannah-Jones and the *New York Times* have yet to respond to these criticisms.

Even the title of the 1619 Project is wrong. As Michael Guasco pointed out in *Smithsonian Magazine* in 2017, years before the 1619 Project was even published, the first slaves arrived in America in 1526, not 1619. Guasco cautions against fixating on 1619, as this ignores the slaves who streamed into American for nearly a century before that year. Arbitrarily picking 1619 as a key year for American history, Guasco says, "effectively erases the memory of more than 500,000 African men, women, and children who had already crossed the Atlantic against their will, aided and abetted Europeans in their endeavors, provided expertise and guidance in a range of enterprises, suffered, died, and—most importantly—endured."[64]

Hannah-Jones admitted as much when she said, "The fight over the 1619 Project is not about history. It is about memory." She then went on to illustrate the dangers of relying on memory, not on facts, by claiming, "I've always said that the 1619 Project is not a history."[65] This is simply not true; just months earlier, Hannah-Jones said on social media, "The 1619 Project is American history, not black history."[66]

But an individual's memory may be faulty. That is why we do not rely on memory when we study history. Instead, we rely on written texts and recorded facts: memories set down in writing and in deeds can therefore be verified and studied.

When we disassociate history—and memory—from facts, we are lost.

Historian Arthur Schlesinger warned about this when he said, "History is to the nation much as the memory is to the individual. The individual who loses his memory doesn't know where he came from or where he's going, and he becomes dislocated and disoriented."[67] The kerfuffle about the 1619 Project, the various retractions, criticisms, restatements, and unhelpful "clarifications"—nothing describes the situation as well as "dislocated" and "disorienting."

The 1619 Project debacle shows just how unimportant facts are to progressives in their quest to rewrite history. But more than facts are on the line here. The entire narrative is false. Tyler O'Neil wrote in a piece for *PJ Media*, "[T]he 1619 Project is also false in a much deeper sense. Its narrative de-legitimizes the very real benefits of American freedom and prosperity by claiming that racist oppression is the central truth behind the country's ideals, while in truth the country was founded in pursuit of freedom and equality, but the Founders allowed slavery to persist, laying the groundwork to defeat it eventually."[68]

Despite its historical inaccuracies and blatant misinformation, the 1619 Project has gained immense popularity. As the editors of *National Review* wrote, "In the blink of an eye, the 1619 Project reoriented the discussion about American history."[69] It earned Nikole Hannah-Jones a Pulitzer Prize. And, even though it is based on unsound scholarship, it is being taught in more than 4,500 schools nationwide.[70] The 1619 Project fits the narrative of those who want to disassociate America from its founding principles. Therefore, it is a useful tool for molding impressionable young people, regardless how distorted it is.

Erwin Lutzer, the former pastor of Moody Church in Chicago, said of the project, "The 1619 Project is a targeted effort intended to show that the United States is to be hated because it's a racist and capitalistic nation whose roots must be destroyed and rebuilt upon a cultural Marxist foundation that will bring equality and justice for all."[71] It does not matter if the project is flawed or even flat-out deceptive. For radical progressives, ideology trumps accuracy.

This is the substance of the Left's efforts to indoctrinate young Americans: to dislocate, disorient, and indoctrinate them with new "memories" with no basis in fact. To create a new reality, one that can be continually shaped and molded to meet the ever-changing demands of contemporary wokeness.

That new reality is not a pretty one. When rioters toppled a statue of George Washington in Portland, Oregon, in the summer of 2020, they spray painted "1619" on it. Hannah-Jones proudly embraced the label, calling the violent mayhem of that summer the "1619 Riots." She said she was honored to claim responsibility for the violent, destructive mobs' behavior[72] and added she seeks nothing less than the "abolition of the United States as we know it."[73]

This is the indoctrination our children face in public schools—even though parents and school boards do not approve. A recent Heritage Foundation survey found 57 percent of parents and 65 percent of school board members do *not* support teaching children the false narrative that America was founded to preserve slavery.

Despite this, the 1619 Project is being taught in thousands of schools across the country, and President Biden's administration cited the 1619 Project as an exemplary piece of work in the new guidelines for Department of Education grants.[74]

Pushing back against the imposition of the 1619 Project from on high, Dennis Prager wrote, "Why would you send your child to any school that teaches *The New York Times'* '1619 Project?' This project holds that America was not founded in 1776 but in 1619, with the arrival of the first black slaves in North America, and that the Revolutionary War was fought not to gain independence from Britain but to preserve slavery. Virtually every leading historian specializing in American history—most of whom are liberals and Democrats, and some of whom were anti-Trump activists—have labeled 'The 1619 Project' a lie."[75]

Prager raises the correct question. Why should we settle for teaching "history" that is not history, for erasing and obscuring the past instead of delving deeper into it? Rather than twisting and mutilating our national story, why are we not seeking to tell that story in a more complete, more compelling, more unifying way?

## ... 1776...

In response to the 1619 Project, former president Donald Trump established the "1776 Commission" to provide a more balanced perspective on our nation's founding. The commission was chaired by Larry Arnn, president of Hillsdale College, and other well-respected and ideologically diverse academics. Its purpose was to outline an alternative to the radical, destructive assertions of partisan journalism like the 1619 Project and, in its own words, to "enable a rising generation to understand the history and principles of the founding of the United States in 1776 and to strive to form a more perfect Union."[76]

That narrative is contrary to the one Leftist historians and activists are imposing throughout our nation's educational system, so of course the 1776 Report came under scathing attack from the media. The report was criticized as lacking in substance and citations, but this criticism overlooked that the commission was only able to release its initial report before it was disbanded by the Biden administration. In other words, the commission released what was essentially an outline of its proposed curriculum, which the media criticized as if it were the completed project.

Journalists at the *New York Times* questioned the "objectivity" and "credentials" of those on the commission,[77] even the 1619 Project's author, Nikole Hannah-Jones, holds no history credentials (she has a masters' degree in journalism). CNN reporter Maegan Vazquez attacked the 1776 Report as a "racist school curriculum report" and a "rebuttal to schools applying a more accurate history curriculum," her euphemism for what Hannah-Jones has called an "origin story" instead of a researched, fact-based history.[78]

Writing in *National Review*, David Harsanyi said, "In fact, CNN offers not a single factual mistake in the Trump commission's paper, only philosophical disagreements. Sometimes you get the sense reporters can't comprehend the difference."[79]

Or perhaps it is not a matter of comprehension. Perhaps instead the progressive media savaged the 1776 Report because the facts of history get in the way of their preferred narrative.

The double standard is telling. The media lauded the 1619 Project despite its author's own admission that it is not a history curriculum; Hannah-Jones responded with ire to the concerns of trained historians; and the project has been shoved into classrooms across the country even though it is factually unsound. The 1776 Report was excoriated as being under researched, though the commission included several historians; it was attacked as being flimsy, even though it was only an initial report, not a whole curriculum; and media stooped to ad hominem attacks on the members of the commission, denouncing them as "racist" with no evidence to support this serious accusation. Regardless the merits of the two projects, the media and governmental response alone shows us there is a serious dearth of objectivity in our national conversation about history.

The commission issued its report on January 18, 2021, the birthday of Rev. Dr. Martin Luther King. The findings in that report neatly delineate the debate going on in our nation today over the teaching of American history and how future generations will understand our past.

Victor Davis Hanson, a prominent historian who was one of the members of the commission, wrote that the report attempts a balanced, rather than slanted, version of America's history. He wrote, "The report does not whitewash the continuance of many injustices after 1776 and 1787—in particular, chattel slavery in the South and voting reserved only for free males. Indeed, the commission explains why and how these wrongs were inconsistent with the letter and spirit of our founding documents. So, it was natural that these disconnects would be addressed throughout our history, even fought over, and continually resolved—often over the opposition of powerful interests who sought to reinvent the Declaration and the Constitution, transforming them into something that they were not."[80]

The report readily acknowledges America and its founders were and are not perfect. It states, "[T]he American story has its share of missteps, errors, contradictions, and wrongs.

These wrongs have always met resistance from the clear principles of the nation, and therefore our history is far more one of self-sacrifice, courage, and nobility . . . . Of course, neither America nor any other nation has perfectly lived up to the universal truths of equality, liberty, justice, and government by consent. But no nation before America ever dared state those truths as the formal basis for its politics, or done more, to achieve them."[81]

The report also addresses the fact America's Founding Fathers set up a system of government designed to lead to the end of slavery, rather than the perpetuation of it. The report states, "The foundation of our Republic planted the seeds of the death of slavery in America. The Declaration's unqualified proclamation of human equality flatly contradicted the existence of human bondage and, along with the Constitution's compromises understood in light of that proposition, set the stage for abolition. Indeed, the movement to abolish slavery that first began in the United States led the way in bringing about the end of legal slavery."[82]

The central disagreement between the 1776 Report and the 1619 Project is not about whether America is a perfect nation. It is about whether the principles and ideals America is founded upon are worth preserving. Here, the methodology of the two projects diverge. The 1619 Project assumes from the beginning the expressed principles of the Founders, contained in the Declaration of Independence and the Constitution of the United States, are a smokescreen. With absolutely no evidence, Hannah-Jones simply assumes America's founding principles are corrupt and not worth preserving.

The 1776 Report, on the other hand, examines the actual language of those principles—language like "life, liberty, and the pursuit of happiness" for all—and finds it worthy. It then proposes a curriculum that studies the actual events of American history considering those principles. From the existence of slavery to our heroic intervention in World War II, from the atrocity of the Trail of Tears to the astonishing American spirit of innovation that has transformed our world, American history is morally complex. The 1776 Report proposes students learn first the ideals on which our nation was founded and develop the critical skills to evaluate whether, in a specific situation, America lived up to her own standards or whether she failed.

Both Frederick Douglass and Rev. Dr. Martin Luther King are mentioned prominently in the report as examples of individuals who challenged our nation to fully realize and enforce the Founders' vision of a nation where all men are created equal.[83] In a piece about the 1776 Report, the editors of *National Review* added, "For [Douglass and King], the words of Jefferson and Madison were the swords and the shields wielded against the enemies of the American creed. To observe the continuity that exists from the victory of 1776 to those of 1865 and 1964 is merely to take great Americans like Douglass and King at their word."[84]

The commission's solution to our nation's current fragmentation is renewed civic education grounded in teaching schoolchildren about our nation's founding documents. Hanson concludes, "[A]ny fair critic can see that the report's unifying message is that we are a people with a singular government and history, that self-critique and moral improvement are innate to the American founding and spirit, and that America never had to be perfect to be good and far better than the alternatives."[85]

The report says,

> The facts of our founding are not partisan. They
> are a matter of history. Controversies about the
> meaning of the founding can begin to be resolved by
> looking at the facts of our nation's founding . . . . The
> principles of the American founding can be learned
> by studying the abundant documents contained in
> the record. Read fully and carefully, they show how
> the American people have ever pursued freedom
> and justice, which are the political conditions for
> living well. To learn this history is to become a better
> person, a better citizen, and a better partner in the
> American experiment in self-government.[86]

Looking at the report's own words, it is clear, criticizing the actions of Americans is a central part of the curriculum the 1776 Commission proposes. We must, to understand our own history clearly, be able to identify the points at which we have failed. This is something parents and school boards across the country agree on; the survey by the Heritage Foundation found 70 percent of parents and 74 percent of school board members believe students should be taught about slavery and curricula should emphasize how much this evil practice harmed individuals and the nation. But the survey also found that parents and school boards believe students should be taught "that freedom and prosperity represent who Americans are as a nation, offering a beacon to those wanting to immigrate here."[87]

In other words, Americans want their children to learn America's ideals are excellent, but we have not always lived up to those ideals. They want young people to know where we have failed and where we have succeeded in protecting and promoting the right to life, liberty, and the pursuit of happiness.

But that is not enough. The Left does not want Americans to be able to articulate when America has failed to meet its own lofty standards; it wants Americans who are brainwashed into denouncing those standards altogether.

On his first day in office, President Joe Biden disbanded the commission, and the 1776 Report was removed from the White House website almost immediately.[88] *National Review* concluded, "That President Biden acted so swiftly against the commission is another sign of how desperately we need voices to combat what is rapidly becoming the new orthodoxy about American history."[89]

So, what is so controversial about the 1776 Report, to get President Biden to take it down from the White House website almost immediately after putting his hand on the Bible and taking the oath of office? To the objective reader, nothing. But to ideologues, the project posed a grave threat. It exposed the mistruths being taught to our schoolchildren; therefore, it had to be shut down.

After "cancelling" the 1776 Report, the Biden White House announced it would offer grants to teach critical race theory and the 1619 Project in public schools (it is already being taught in more than 4,500 schools), knowing that cash-strapped public schools will usually take grants no matter what strings are attached. According to the administration, the goal of the grants is to "improve the teaching of American history, civics, and government in elementary schools and secondary schools, including the teaching of traditional American history,"[90] even though the 1619 Project is, even according to its author, explicitly not history.

Those pushing the reinterpretations of our history have gone as far as threatening teachers with fines and punishment if they do not comply. This is what happened in Loudoun County, Virginia, after the school district adapted a program to "enhance the low level of racial consciousness and racial literacy" of its faculty. The district included a list of punishments for any teacher who questioned the policy, even in a private capacity.[91] This same school district went on to "cancel" Dr. Seuss because one possible reading of some of his books does not conform to the current cultural orthodoxy.[92]

The situation in California is even worse. As I mentioned earlier, In 2020, the state Department of Education created a model curriculum so extreme it even left some Left-wing legislators aghast. According to the Education Department website, the new semester-long ethnic studies class (launching in 2025) will "build new possibilities for post-imperial life that promotes collective narratives of transformative resistance." That is classic Orwellian speak.

The curriculum prescribes teaching "the four 'I's of oppression: ideological, institutional, interpersonal, and internalized. It mandates students participate in political activities, regardless their own convictions, with the goal of turning schoolchildren into "positive actors in their communities to address a contemporary issue and present findings in a public forum." The "approved" issues students can address include "racism, LGBTQ rights, immigration rights, access to quality health care, [and] income inequality."[93] There is a vast amount of disagreement within our society on these issues, but the course would not equip students to come to their own conclusions on these questions. Instead, it prescribes an opinion and requires students to lobby politically for that opinion, whether they share it or not.

Even the nation's number one high school, Thomas Jefferson High School for Science and Technology in Fairfax County, Virginia, has gotten into the act. Parents were not allowed to have any input in a new curriculum and only found out about its radicalism when their children came home and told them about it. The curriculum, meant to shame students who have been successful, advances a false narrative pitting groups against each other rather than bringing them together. After the school told concerned parents the curriculum change was a student-led initiative, parents did some investigating. They found out the curriculum was mandated by school officials who simply informed the students it would be implemented.[94]

This kind of top-down enforcement of curricula parents, students, and school boards alike do not want should come as no surprise.

Progressive school officials and activists see parents and school boards as the enemy and are determined to drive a wedge between parents and their children. Far too many parents are unaware of what their children are being taught in school. Then parents are mystified when children reach their teens and reject the values their parents tried to instill in them. If somehow a young person makes it through K-12 with her respect for her parents intact, she is then handed over to a public university that sets about convincing her to reject the values and beliefs of her "close-minded" parents.

Erwin Lutzer, who I quoted earlier, describes the ultimate goals of those who seek to destroy America's past, writing, "The destruction of monuments is part of a larger attempt to destroy what it means to be an American. It's an attempt to remove not just racism, but to discredit all else that was done by those who created our nation's foundational principles that led to making America what it is. In the minds of many people, America is so terrible it cannot be fixed; it must be destroyed and rebuilt according to a radical socialist agenda."[95]

This effort must begin with rewriting history.

The British journalist, poet, and novelist G. K. Chesterton once said, "About half the history now taught in schools and colleges is made windy and barren by the narrow notion of leaving out the theological theories . . . . Historians seem to have completely forgotten two facts—First, that men act from ideas; and second, that it might, therefore, be as well to discover which ideas."[96]

Citing Chesterton, Joseph Pearce wrote in *The Imaginative Conservative*:

> Properly understood, history is a chronological map that shows us not only where we have come from but also where we are, and how we got here. It is also possible to project where we are likely to be going in the future by drawing the line of knowledge on the chronological map from where we have come from to where we are now and extending the line into the realm of future possibilities. In this sense history can also be a prophet. It increases our knowledge of the past, present, and future. This, however, is only true if the chronological map is accurate. If it has been drawn by those with prejudiced perceptions or a prejudiced agenda, it will only succeed in getting us lost. There are few things more dangerous than an inaccurate map, especially if we find ourselves in perilous terrain. . . .
>
> The tragedy of modern education, perceived with such brilliance by Chesterton, is that it has left

us perilously ignorant of who we are, where we are, where we have come from, and where we are going. We are lost and blissfully unaware that we are heading for the abyss. Such is the price we are doomed to pay for our blind faith in nothing in particular.[97]

Without that chronological map or without an accurate chronological map, we, as a nation, have no direction. We know neither where we have come from nor where we are going. We wander aimlessly from one theory to another, getting more and more lost and disoriented when, if we would only stop and look backward—honestly and humbly—at where we came from, we would be able to decide where we are going.

Even amid all the turmoil, some Americans are trying to do just that. Remember the 1776 Commission? Even though the commission was barred from acting in a government capacity, in May 2021 it announced it would be continuing its work under the auspices of Hillsdale College.[98] In its press release, the commission wrote, "The restoration of American education can only be grounded in a history of America and its principles that is accurate, honest, unifying, inspiring, and ennobling." It urges mothers and fathers to take charge of their children's civic and historical education. It urges concerned citizens to run for election to school boards and city councils, where they can have immediate positive influence on what is taught in local schools.

Finally, the commission said, "recalling the long history of citizen participation in our civic life, we call on states, counties, and local communities to form their own 1776 Commissions to advance this great work of American renewal as we prepare for the 250th anniversary of the Declaration of Independence in July 2026."[99]

Later in the book, I will address a few other ways we can help our children and, ultimately, our society pause, look, learn, and orient themselves regarding the past.

But before we can offer a solution, we must further examine the root of the problem. That root is Howard Zinn, among other revisionist historians, who have turned our children not against their country but, in some cases, against their own families.

# 3

# *Original Zinn*

*Civil disobedience is not our problem.*
*Our problem is civil obedience.*[1]

HOWARD ZINN

*We need to get accustomed to the idea that*
*there will be more Communist countries in the world,*
*and that this is not necessarily bad.*[2]

HOWARD ZINN

*The political history of the United States . . .*
*is in large measure a history of almost unthinkable brutality*
*towards slaves; genocidal hatred of Native Americans,*
*racist devaluation of nonwhites and nonwhite cultures,*
*sexual devaluation of women.*[3]

ROBIN WEST

*In many schools, you are more likely to encounter the 1619*
*Project or Zinn version of history than anything positive. We're*
*telling our young people that America is racist and oppressive*
*and has only failed over the years to do the right thing by*
*the most vulnerable, rather than that we were founded with*
*incredible ideals that we have sometimes failed to live up to.*[4]

MICHAEL J. PETRILLI

∼∼∾

The godfather of the radical attack on America's history and heritage is the late Howard Zinn. Zinn was an academic; he served as chair of history and social science at Spelman College and professor of history at Boston University. He was a writer, penning more than twenty books and a play about Emma Goldman. And he has become one of the greatest influences on American young people for decades, through his best-selling 1980 book *A People's History of the United States*, a socialist reimagining of American history.

While the influence of Zinn and his fellow Leftist propagandists had already infiltrated America's academic institutions decades earlier, it was his epic screed *A People's History* that led to the rapid acceleration of deliberate distortions of American history to turn future generations against their country.

*A People's History* has become a popular supplemental book in high schools, and Zinn wrote a companion volume (*A Young People's History of the United States*) in 2009. In an email interview with *Politifact* in April 2015, Grant T. Sewall of the American Textbook Council said, while it is impossible to determine how many teachers use Zinn's books in their classrooms, Zinn's impact on social studies teachers is prodigious and possibly unparalleled."[5]

Zinn singlehandedly transformed the study of history in American public education from the discipline of surveying facts and events to the display of "reframing" and "reimagining" facts to fit a particular narrative. The astonishing acceptance of *A People's History* paved the way for historically unsound work like the 1619 Project to succeed despite its blatant inaccuracies.

Zinn said from the beginning he wanted to "transform" American history by writing about those he perceived to be "underdogs." This in itself is not a flawed project; historians tend to look first at the actions and motivations of a small group of influential figures, and there is much historical gold to be mined from the day-to-day lives and choices of ordinary people.

But Zinn did not have a merely historical project of depicting what less-lofty Americans were thinking, saying, and doing. He said his goal was to denounce Western civilization and to convince students to reject it, marred as he said it was "by the religion of popes, the government of kings, the frenzy of money."[6] Zinn had a political and a moral project in mind: To invert all the power structures of America, past and present, a task requiring him to defame the Founders and many other American leaders and institutions as well as upend the social and moral foundations of our country.

Zinn did not go as far as Nikole Hannah-Jones in denouncing the very principles on which our nation was founded. In a 2007 letter to the *New York Times*, Zinn wrote, "I want young people to understand that ours is a beautiful country, but it has been taken over by men who have no respect for human rights or constitutional liberties. Our people are basically decent and caring, and our highest ideals are expressed in the Declaration of Independence, which says that all of us have an equal right to 'life, liberty, and the pursuit of happiness.'"[7]

Here we see Zinn invoking the principles of America's founding and expressing some respect for the Declaration of

Independence. But we also see his basic project at work. When Zinn says, "[Our country] has been taken over by men who have no respect for human rights or constitutional liberties," he is referring not only to contemporary leaders but to the Founding Fathers, who he accused of agitating for the Revolutionary War as a power-grab to perpetuate inequalities in the states. He sets up the assumption that all groups or ideas gaining political or social power obtained that power through oppressing other groups or ideas. That lays the ground for him to issue a sweeping condemnation of the Founding Fathers, as well as their Judeo-Christian convictions. So when Zinn said America is a beautiful country and expresses admiration for our founding principles, his words ring hollow because he believed the entire government system of the United States has been oppressive and exploitive since the beginning.

Krystina Skurk, a press assistant at the U.S. House of Representatives and a researcher for Hillsdale College's Kirby Center, wrote for *The Federalist*, "Most of the debates in the public square today have been influenced one way or another by Zinn's ideology hidden in the guise of history."[8]

## IGNORING STANDARDS TO PROMOTE IDEOLOGY

In a recent scholarly criticism of Zinn's work titled *Debunking Howard Zinn*, Dr. Mary Grabar writes, *A People's History* "is more than another Left-wing interpretation of history . . . . Zinn's propaganda has been spectacularly effective. His dishonest American history is not the only factor in Americans' turn away from their heritage of freedom towards communist fantasies . . . but he has been instrumental in this destructive transformation."[9]

And Dr. Grabar knows just how deadly Zinn's "communist fantasies" can be, as she was born in Communist Yugoslavia. When she was just a baby, her parents escaped from the country, avoiding Communist border guards, and fleeing to Austria. They then immigrated to the United States when Dr. Grabar was two.[10] She has spent years working to preserve America's heritage of freedom in academia, founding the Dissident Prof Education Project and writing tirelessly against the Leftist effort to discredit America. Dr. Grabar writes, "According to Zinn, there's no such thing as objective history, anyway: [he writes] 'the historian's distortion is more than technical, it is ideological; it is released into a world of contending interests, where any chosen emphasis supports (whether the historian means to or not) some kind of interest, whether economic or political or racial or national, or sexual.'"[11]

This view is parent to Nikole Hannah-Jones's "history as memory" view, in which shoddy journalism is as credible as careful historical research. To Zinn, morality demands he manipulate history to fit his narrative; standards of historical analysis are merely "technical problems" to be dismissed.[12]

Grabar says through sleight-of-hand, consisting of "outlandish suggestions and grossly dishonest rhetorical tricks . . . Howard Zinn has succeeded in convincing a generation of Americans that the nation Abraham Lincoln truly called 'the last best hope on Earth' is essentially a racist criminal enterprise built on murdering Indians, exploiting slaves, and oppressing the working man."[13]

Grabar is critical not merely of Zinn's conclusions but of his methodology. She shows how Zinn begins with his own presupposition—America's real history is one of oppression and tyranny—and proceeds to distort the historical record to fit that presupposition.

Zinn is open about his project from the beginning of *A People's History*, where he says, "I prefer to tell the story of the discovery of America from the viewpoint of the Arawaks, the Constitution from the standpoint of the slaves, of Andrew Jackson as seen by the Cherokees, of the Civil War as seen by the New York Irish."[14]

These are truly interesting historical questions: How did the Arawaks perceive the coming of Columbus? What did the New York Irish think about the Civil War? But they are questions of perception obligating a historian to ground his research in plenty of evidence, documentation, and facts. These questions, when properly researched and reported, can enhance our understanding of a certain period. They are not questions that should revolutionize our understanding of that period simply because probing these questions does not change the facts; it deepens the way we understand those facts, but it does not change them.

Zinn is not content with that. He does not want to deepen our understanding of a historical period; he wants to upend it, and to do that, he must supply new facts to fit his narrative. As someone with deep Communist sympathies, Zinn believed the U.S. Constitution was written to protect the interests of a wealthy elite.[15] In true Marxist fashion, he castigates the Declaration of Independence for not addressing "property inequality."[16]

While Zinn denied he was a member of the Communist Party, eyewitness accounts of Zinn at Communist Party gatherings indicate he at the very least had strong sympathy for the movement. The *Communist Manifesto* declares, "the history of all hitherto existing society is the history of class struggle."[17] Zinn echoes this, saying, "[That principle is] undeniably true, verifiable in any reading of history.

Certainly true for the United States, despite all the promises of the Constitution."[18]

Zinn, in his autobiography, explains his goal was to portray the Founding Fathers as "rich white slaveholders" and to depict our military heroes and presidents in a negative light—in particular Jefferson, Lincoln (who Zinn describes as "a cowardly, racist politician beholden to powerful money interests"[19] who initiated hostilities with the South[20]), Wilson, Franklin Roosevelt (who Zinn says waged World War II to benefit the "wealthy elite"[21]), and Kennedy—as being "more concerned with political power and national aggrandizement than rights of non-white people."[22]

Dr. Mary Grabar points out how Zinn's approach is against the American Historical Association's standards of Professional Use Conduct. Those standards state:

1. Historians should document their findings and be prepared to make available their sources, evidence, and data, including any documentation, through interviews.
2. Historians should not misrepresent their sources.
3. They should report their findings as accurately as possible and not omit evidence that runs counter to their own interpretation.
4. They should not commit plagiarism.
5. They should oppose false or erroneous use of evidence, along with any efforts to ignore or conceal such false or erroneous use.[23]

She writes of *A People's History*, "On page after page, I found use of dubious sources, plagiarism, misrepresentations of authors' meanings, withholding of critical information, logical and emotional fallacies, and rhetoric suitable to propaganda, which ultimately is what the book is. The solutions for the inevitable failures of the American system to which Zinn points always lie in socialism."[24]

Grabar also writes, "According to Zinn, there's no such thing as objective history, anyway."[25] She then offers the following quote from him: "[T]he historian's distortion is more than technical, it is ideological; it is released into a world of contending interests, where any chosen emphasis supports (whether the historian means to or not). Whether economic or political or racial or national or sexual."[26]

She adds, "Once ideology has become a moral virtue, Zinn can discount standards of scholarship—such as those of the American Historical Association—as having to do with nothing more important than 'technical problems of excellence'—standards of no importance compared to his kind of history, which consists in forging 'tools for contending social classes, races, nations.'"[27]

Zinn makes the following arguments with little or no documentation to back them up, thereby violating the American Historical Association's standards. Nevertheless, his work is seen by many as the "gold standard" to be taught to impressionable schoolchildren and young adults.

Grabar points out how Zinn added ellipses to sentences from Columbus's diaries while removing entire sections, thereby changing Columbus's intent to share his Christian faith with the Indians through love, not force.[28] Interestingly, Zinn's critique of Columbus closely resembles that of Karl Marx and Frederick Engels, the founders of communism, who accused Columbus of ushering in the "bourgeoisie" through the initiation of commerce.[29]

Another classic example of Zinn's deliberate misinformation is his treatment of the Pilgrims, who gave us the

Mayflower Compact, the document upon which our Declaration of Independence and, ultimately, the U.S. Constitution were based—guaranteeing us the freedoms we enjoy today—as practitioners of genocide.

But here is the truth about the Mayflower Compact, as recorded by numerous respected historians.

On November 11, 1620, the Pilgrims, along with others who came along for the journey, arrived on the Massachusetts shore after sailing across the Atlantic Ocean in a leaky and overcrowded ship rife with disease, with the hope of coming to a new world where they could freely practice their faith and exercise their rights of conscience. They had no intentions of engaging in cultural genocide.

Once they arrived in Massachusetts, the Pilgrims and others realized they needed a system of government for their new home. They created the Mayflower Compact, which recognized people derived their right of self-government from God and not man. It was the first attempt at self-government on the North American continent—an attempt that has been successful for four hundred years.

While the document used Christianity as its base and said all colonists should live in accordance with the Christian faith, it was also a pluralistic document meant for the good of both Christians and non-Christians alike to be able to govern themselves and live in harmony with each other. It stated the colonists would create and enact "laws, ordinances, acts, constitutions, and offices" that would allow the colony to thrive, and they would create one society and work with each other, rather than in opposition to each other, because faith informs good government for all.

In 1820, at the commemoration of the 200th anniversary of the Pilgrims' arrival at Plymouth, the orator Daniel

Webster spoke of the great legacy given to all Americans by the Pilgrims, encouraging the Americans of that day to offer future Americans "some proof that we have endeavored to transmit the great inheritance unimpaired; that in our estimate of public principles and private virtue, in our veneration of religion and piety, in our devotion to civil and religion's liberty, in our regard for whatever advances human knowledge or improves human happiness, we are not altogether unworthy of its origin."[30]

In fact, the legacy Webster describes, is exactly the principles put to paper by Thomas Jefferson and the signers of the Declaration of Independence, as Webster went on to talk about how the values of the Pilgrims were instrumental in laying the foundation upon which our nation was built. Those foundations were self-government, private property, Christian morals, industry, and religious liberty. Webster went on to denounce slavery as a "shame" against the heritage bequeathed by the Pilgrims.[31]

Sadly, thanks to the efforts of Howard Zinn, the 1619 Project, and others who have rewritten American history, our nation has departed from the ideals of the Mayflower Compact and subsequently our nation's other founding documents. As Jarrett Stepman has written, "[I]t is impossible to separate America from its profoundly religious, mostly Protestant Christian origin as some modern, Left-wing historians have tried to do. Efforts to purge Christianity and religion from American public life are not true to our nation's heritage."[32]

Later in *A People's History*, Zinn doubles down on the motives of those who founded our nation, and his words have likely led to other historical distortions such as the 1619 Project and critical race theory. Writing about the Founding Fathers, Zinn says the founders created the United States as a legal entity that "could take over land, profits, and political power from favorites of the British Empire." He adds, "In the process, they could hold back a number of potential rebellions and create a consensus of popular support for the rule of a new, privileged leadership."[33]

Zinn also mocks those who fought and, in many cases, gave their lives in World War II to protect the world against Adolf Hitler and fascism, stating we only entered the war because we wanted to advance, in his words, "the imperial interests of the United States," not because we were trying to stop the wholesale slaughter of European Jews.[34]

But it does not end there. Zinn calls into doubt America's involvement in World War II, calling Japan a victim of "American aggression" (conveniently forgetting the attack on Pearl Harbor) and Nazi Germany, which exterminated six million Jews, as no worse than the Allied Forces[35] who liberated those remaining from the concentration camps so horrific General George Patton, one of the toughest warriors of all time, vomited when he saw the human carnage in those camps.

He goes on to state the Marshall Plan, in which America spent billions of dollars to rebuild Europe after World War II, was nothing more than an effort to "create a network of American corporate control over the globe" (yet brought incredible prosperity to Europe and Japan).

Finally, Zinn states, the Vietnam War was a "modern day David vs. Goliath story with the giant imperialistic power justly humiliated."[36]

But Zinn's flaws run even deeper than historical; he makes the most juvenile of all academic errors that, if he'd made it in a college course, would have earned him a failing grade: plagiarism. Speaking at a Heritage Foundation event, Grabar said, in *A People's History*, "In terms of Columbus, [Zinn] mostly copied from passages quoted in a book he plagiarized, a book for high school students written by a fellow Marxist and anti-war Vietnam War organizer who was not a historian, but a novelist by the name of Hans Koning."[37]

As the saying goes, if you repeat a lie enough times, it becomes the truth, as University of Massachusetts professor James Green pointed out, when he said, "nearly every college textbook published during the last two decades now begins, as Zinn did, with the European destruction of the Indians."[38]

I would be amiss if I did not say there were Europeans who came to America who treated the Native American tribes horribly. But Zinn, and his fellow Leftist historians, have made the entire story about America's founding, such as Nikole Hannah-Jones has done with the 1619 Project. By focusing on selective injustices that occurred, rather than the entire story, and defaming those who acted heroically in the context of their times, this "re-interpretation" of American history has only succeeded in dividing, rather than uniting us, as a country.

True historians see this problem, as it is not only conservatives who criticize Howard Zinn; much of the best criticism of *A People's History* has come from academics on the Left who see Zinn as a threat not merely to America but to the discipline of history as a whole. Arthur Schlesinger, the liberal historian I discussed earlier, characterized Zinn as a "polemicist, not a historian."[39]

Avowed Marxist historian Eugene Genovese thought Zinn's book was so bad he refused to review it.[40] Cultural historian Michael Kammen labeled Zinn's work, "a scissors-and-paste-pot-job."[41] Their criticisms are based on much of what I have already mentioned—a disregard for professional standards, taking events out of context to advance a political narrative, and using rhetorical devices rather than facts to manipulate his reader's opinions.

The last criticism is a point made by Sam Wineburg of Stanford University, who has led the charge against Zinn's work from the liberal perspective. He writes, *A People's History* is so radical in its rhetoric as well as its politics that it is "educationally dangerous."[42]

Wineburg pointed out this quote from Zinn's chapter on World War II: "With the defeat of the Axis, were fascism's essential elements—militarism, racism, imperialism—now gone? Or were they absorbed into the already poisoned bones of the victors?" Wineburg explains this is not historical analysis; it is vicious political commentary intended to turn students against their own country. Zinn's book does not teach the facts but instead tries to convince the reader to question the motives of those who fought to preserve our freedom and liberate those being oppressed and slaughtered.

As Dr. Grabar writes, by posing his political beliefs in the form of a rhetorical question, Zinn can suggest the United States is the moral equivalent of Nazi Germany without having to offer any evidence for that claim.[43] *A People's History* has indeed absorbed the poison of communism and socialism and is willing to corrupt historical record to leach that poison into its readers.

Wineburg criticizes Zinn's style of writing, which appeals directly to student's hearts instead of their minds. He says such appeals to *pathos* without critical thought is dangerous because it "extinguishes students' ability to think." And, as Wineburg points out, "for many students, *A People's History* will be the first full-length history book they read, and for some, it will be the only one."[44]

Wineburg is far from the only liberal critic of Zinn. Writing in the *New Republic* (hardly a conservative publication), David Greenberg excoriated *A People's History* as "a pretty lousy piece of work." Greenberg bemoans the wide influence of Zinn's book, writing, "the shifts that the radical historians of the 1960s triggered were diverse enough to defy encapsulation." Despite the widespread denunciation of *A People's History* by credible historians, the book's "transgressive vapors still beguile young minds." Greenberg concludes, "To be sure, when they get to college, many of these students continue to read books, including works of history. And some of them come to realize that Zinn's famous book is . . . a pretty lousy piece of work."[45] But many students never come to that realization because they have been fully indoctrinated in Zinn's ideology before they have developed the critical thinking skills to see through Zinn's manipulations of history.

## THE TRAGIC LEGACY OF HOWARD ZINN

Fast forward to the present day, a record number of young adults are embracing socialism while rejecting capitalism. A 2019 poll found 61 percent of Americans aged between eighteen and twenty-four have a positive reaction to the word *socialism* compared to 58 percent for *capitalism*.[46] Socialism has become romanticized by Zinn and his peers, while capitalism, albeit imperfect like all man-made systems, is demonized.

These are the same young adults who are defacing and defaming those who discovered America and fought for her independence and freedom. A recent poll done by the Harvard Kennedy School of Government found that 37 percent of college students described themselves as either "not very patriotic" or "not patriotic at all."[47] Is it any wonder, given the pervasiveness of Zinn's radical anti-American ideology at all levels of our educational system?

Former U.S. Senator Orrin Hatch perhaps put it best when he wrote, "Texts of dubious historical accuracy—including *The New York Times* 1619 Project and Howard Zinn's 'A People's History of the United States'—have damaged the teaching of social studies and civics in secondary education. By focusing almost exclusively on our nation's sins, these texts give students a jaded view of history and take little to no account of the indispensable role the United States has played in securing freedom, democracy and human rights around the globe . . . . Students will never love a country they've been taught to despise."[48]

Zinn's book has generated a religious fervor among its adherents. It is so revered by Leftist activists it replaced the Bible at a swearing-in ceremony for one Oklahoma City council member.[49]

And that is what Zinn intended. His ultimate goal is not a historical one but a political one: he wanted to depict the United States as an illegitimate enterprise, one demanding a revolution. In *A People's History*, Zinn denied the United States even exists, saying all that holds America together is a shared pretense about our own existence. "The pretense is that there really is such a thing as 'the United States,' subject to occasional conflicts and quarrels, but fundamentally a community of people with common interests. It is as if there really is a 'national interest' represented in the Constitution, in territorial expansion, in the laws passed by Congress, the decisions of the courts, the development of capitalism, the culture of education, and the mass media."[50]

There seems to be no escaping Howard Zinn's ideology. Mary Grabar writes, while Zinn was not much of a scholar or historian, he did mesmerize his students as a political activist. Instead of using textbooks or standard history books, he had his students read poetry, fiction, drama, and polemics.[51] As a teacher, he did not appear particularly concerned about whether his students learned anything, as he never gave exams and did not require his students to use footnotes in their papers to document their research. He did, however, require his students to be involved in "community organizing." Basically, he was teaching his students his own personal disregard for professional standards.

An example of how the influence of Zinn and his followers goes beyond the mere teaching of history, it is infecting all other aspects of a child's education as well, as freelance writer and editor Beth Feeley[52] discovered when her children attended school remotely during the COVID-19 pandemic.

One day, Feeley's high school-aged son asked her to look at a reading assignment from his world history class about parents raising "theybies," i.e., genderless children. The next day, her son received an assignment in another class: the assignment summarized the critical race theory before requiring him to read an article on how black singer Lil Nas X's song "Old Town Road" was removed from the country music charts. This assignment was from his physics class! What Lil Nas X has to do in a class dealing with verifiable science, rather than interpretation of facts, is a mystery.[53]

We see Zinn's victimhood version of history at work in these assignments. Zinn moves us from e pluribus unum (one from many) to a philosophy of everyone out for him or herself as it pits one group against another—and it ends up infecting all levels of the educational system—even physics, which has little to do with history. For all the yearning comments for "unity" from the political Left, you cannot have unity when every group has a grievance against another group.

Fred Siegel, associate professor of history at Cooper Union and a self-identified liberal Democrat, wrote in 1991, "[The new historians see America] as a story of defeat, despair, and domination. American history became a tragedy in three acts: what we did to the Indians, what we did to the Blacks, and what we did to everyone else."[54] Dr. Mary Grabar says, "That's a pretty fair description of *A People's History of the United States* . . . .[55] Zinn," Grabar writes, "will do anything to make America look bad."[56]

As Joy Pullman, writing for *The Federalist*, put it, "[N]ot only is Zinn's book a pack of slipshod lies that even Leftist historians will not stand behind, it is a pack of slipshod lies that appear to be told purposefully to set Americans at each other's throats. And it has been quite effective. Many Americans believe the false and self-immolating narrative that their nation is fundamentally and unreformably racist, sexist, and genocidal."[57]

That is the work of Howard Zinn and his advocates over the past forty years—that, and the polarized nation America has become, in which discourse is impossible and unity seems a distant dream.

# 4

# *Divided We Fall*

*It's a universal law—intolerance is the first sign
of an inadequate education. An ill-educated person
behaves with arrogant impatience, whereas
a truly profound education breeds humility.*[1]

ALEXANDER SOLZHENITSYN

*The culture wars are not really about right vs. left;
they are about memory versus oblivion.*[2]

BENJAMIN MYERS

*Truth does not become more true by virtue of the fact
that the entire world agrees with it, nor less so
even if the whole world disagrees with it.*[3]

MOSES MAIMONIDES

*A house divided against itself cannot stand. I believe this
government cannot endure, permanently half slave and half
free. I do not expect the Union to be dissolved—I do not expect
the house to fall—but I do expect it will cease to be divided. It
will become all one thing or all the other.*[4]

ABRAHAM LINCOLN

In the past several years, looking out at the violence, hate, and disunity dominating our public discourse, many of us find ourselves asking, "What's happened to America?"

I hear this question often from friends and family members who remember an America where we were civil to each other regardless our differences—whether spiritual, political, or economic. An America where Democrats worshipped at the same churches with Republicans, where friends and neighbors stopped in the aisle of the local grocery store to catch up and talk about family instead of politics, where schoolchildren were taught about the greatness of their country and about their responsibility to make their country the best it could be.

This America is gone thanks, in part, to the efforts of "historians" such as Howard Zinn.

From the rioting, looting, and destruction in our inner cities to the attacks upon our national and state governing institutions; from lesson plans excoriating America's founding principles to political leaders who denounce our nation's core values—the days when we were a nation with a shared sense of the common good are an increasingly distant memory.

For example, a 2020 Pew Research study found a month before the presidential election, roughly eight in ten registered voters in both camps said their political disagreements with others were about core American values, with roughly nine in ten—liberals and conservatives—worried about a victory by the other would lead to "lasting harm" to the United States.[5]

Thomas Carothers and Andrew O'Donohue, authors of the book *Democracies Divided*, state our country's polarization runs particularly deep in the U.S. in part because American polarization is "especially multifaceted." They write about a "powerful alignment of ideology, race, and religion renders America's divisions unusually encompassing and profound. It is hard to find another example of polarization in the world fusing all three major types of identity divisions in a similar way."[6]

It is not a stretch of the imagination to propose the teaching of American history focusing on victimhood and division has contributed mightily to this polarization.

More studies prove this out. In 2018, a Public Religion Research Institute (PRRI) poll found 47 percent of Americans believed our nation has changed so much they felt "like a stranger in their own country." Nearly six in ten Republicans now felt alienated because of all the changes that have occurred, compared to four in ten Democrats. The PRRI commented on the findings, "The survey finds that partisans see two entirely different American futures."[7]

The current issues pitting neighbor against neighbor, friend against friend, and family member against family member are the result of the war on our values, history, and heritage. The front lines of that war are the classrooms of America as we have seen recently with the advancement of the critical race theory—the foundation of the 1619 Project—and the mandate that all children be subjected to learning about how their country is an oppressor rather than liberator. This mandate has come down from practically every educational power-broker, whether it be the current administration or the powerful National Education Association, which has vowed to fight back against parents who object to its teaching and which only seeks to divide us even more as a nation.[8]

The divisions we see today are strikingly similar to those preceding the American Civil War. The 1776 Commission wrote about these similarities in its report, stating, "[T]he damage done by the denial of core American principles [leading up to the Civil War] and by the attempted substitution of a theory of group rights in their place proved widespread and long-lasting. These, indeed, are the direct ancestors of some of the destructive theories that today divide our people and tear at the fabric of our country."[9]

## How the Teaching of History Impacts American Discourse

In his book *The Fractured Republic*, Yuval Levin writes how this divide has negatively impacted our country: "The melting pot was not working nearly as well in the late twentieth century America as it had a century earlier . . . . With the decline of a strong and coherent national identity, many Americans—especially those belonging to ethnic minority groups—naturally sought to emphasize subnational identities. So, while individualism might have been the driving force behind the nation's cultural deconsolidation, it resulted in the emergence of a politics of group rights and multiculturalism."[10]

Joseph Loconte, writing in *National Review*, adds, "[T]he minds of many conservatives today are focused on another great task: defeating the progressive attack on our constitutional order and the moral legitimacy of the American Founding. Indeed, the ascendance of the progressive Left in politics and culture, and now the fury that has engulfed parts of the Right, can have only one result: an even more embittered and fractious society."[11]

What we are witnessing as the result of the "reinterpretation" of our history by Zinn and others is increased tribalism on the Left and the Right, each with their own distorted views of our history and system of government—views fueled by ignorance or by demagogues, again on the Left and the Right, preying upon that ignorance to advance their own agendas.

Besides conservatives, liberals are also sounding the alarm—especially regarding "cancelling" individuals with whom we disagree. This "cancelling" often takes a silent form, where people are afraid to say anything in fear of being attacked from either side of the political spectrum. Bari Weiss, whom I mentioned earlier, wrote how this self-censorship is a threat to our constitutional republic. She says,

> The liberal worldview that we took for granted in the West from the end of the Cold War until a few years ago is under siege. It came under siege on the right by the rapid spread of internet cults and conspiracy theories . . . . On the left, liberalism is under siege by a new, illiberal orthodoxy that has taken root all around, including in the very institutions meant to uphold the liberal order. And cancellation is this ideology's most effective weapon. It uses cancellation in the way ancient societies used witch burnings: to strike fear into the hearts of everyone watching.[12]

The result is a poisonous clash of worldviews. Those who hold a Christian worldview find themselves at odds with numerous secular worldviews—several that are grounded in Marxism—which use the guise of "economic inequality" or "systemic racism" to play to people's natural sin nature to be envious of others.

And what else does Marxism take advantage of? Revisionist history and "cancelling people" from history, as we are seeing played out daily. It seeks to divide, rather than unite people. For Marxism, and its goal of a powerful, centralized government to take hold, it must create an "us vs. them" mentality, which means creating the conditions for a well-ordered society to descend into chaos. Once chaos has taken over, people are much more prone to give in to Marxist ideas for the sake of "peace."

Given how the teachings of radical Leftist historians have infected our entire culture and robbed us of our national identity, it is no accident America is where she is today—a tattered and bloodied version of her best self. The only way unity can be restored is if one side waves the white flag of surrender.

Bari Weiss adds, "The consensus view [before cancel culture] relied on a few foundational truths that seemed obvious as the blue of the sky: the belief that everyone is created in the image of God; the belief that everyone is equal because of it; the presumption of innocence; a revulsion to mob justice; a commitment to pluralism and free speech, and to liberty of thought and of faith."[13]

Weiss goes on to say the worldview binding as a nation was not blood or soil but a commitment to a shared set of ideas. Once you remove that commitment, there is nothing left to keep the nation together. She writes, "This old consensus—every single aspect of it—has been run over by a new illiberal orthodoxy. Because this ideology cloaks itself in the language of progress, many understandably fall for its self-branding. Don't. It promises revolutionary justice, but it threatens to drag us back into the mean of history, in which we are pitted against one another according to tribe."[14]

Thus, as Weiss writes, we have reverted to a society where it is the interests of one "tribe" against those of another "tribe," and there can be no satisfaction until one or the other tribe has been utterly humiliated and completely defeated. Thanks to Zinn and his colleagues, we are now engaged in a cultural zero-sum game where the ultimate loser is the system of government and civil society intended by our Founding Fathers, as well as the American people. The result is America is *regressing*, not progressing.

We now have an America divided against itself, where "blue states" war against "red states," the secular war with the religious, and the patriotic war against those who believe, like Howard Zinn and others, that America is fatally flawed and inherently corrupt. And the results, as seen by the polls mentioned earlier and through the media talking heads of our day, are sobering.

Victor Davis Hanson, writing in *National Review*, says, "Americans are increasingly either proud of past U.S. traditions, ongoing reform, and current American exceptionalism, or they insist that the country was hopelessly flawed at birth and must be radically reinvented to rectify its original sins."[15]

These findings and statements are the bitter fruit of Howard Zinn and historical atrocities such as the 1619 Project.

What is particularly troubling is how this breaks out over generational lines, with younger generations more likely to agree with Howard Zinn that America was flawed at birth and must be radically reinvented. This is reflected in the statistics I shared earlier on how younger generations are far less likely to be patriotic than those who were raised before the teaching of history was either ignored or co-opted by Zinn and his followers.

But it also goes back to the point of the Solzhenitsyn quote I shared at the beginning of the chapter, which is a growing intolerance to any view except one's own, which is a sign of an inadequate education. This intolerance plays out on both ends of the ideological spectrum, whether it be because of revisionist teaching of history in our nation's schools, colleges, and universities or because history and civics is not taught at all, especially in grades K-12. The resulting cancel culture in which any view, whether it be liberal or conservative, opposing one's own must be silenced, and in many cases, punished, has poisoned our national discourse and turned neighbor against neighbor.

Chief Justice of the United States Supreme Court John Roberts raised his concern about America's failing civic education in his 2019 letter accompanying his annual report on the work of the federal courts. Roberts wrote, "Every generation has an obligation to pass on to the next, not only a fully functioning government responsive to the needs of the people, but the tools to understand and improve it. . . . [W]e have come to take democracy for granted, and civic education has fallen by the wayside. In our age, when social media can instantly spread rumor and false information on a grand scale, the public's need to understand our government, and the protections it provides is even more vital."[16]

Without civic education, chaos ensues, as many Americans have no idea of the freedoms the Constitution provides (which I discussed earlier) and how our system of government works. Pile on historical distortions and the defaming of those founders of our system of government, and you have a toxic brew of social unrest where emotions and vitriol replace facts and civil discourse.

In 1974, the late Irving Kristol wrote about the legacy of virtue, as bequeathed us by our nation's founders, sorely needed to be restored. Now, nearly fifty years later, the urgency for such a restoration is even greater.

According to Kristol, and as I discussed earlier, what the Founding Fathers created was based on the same concept as the Mayflower Compact: a system of self-government requiring, as he put it, the "curbing of one's passions and moderating one's opinions to achieve a large consensus that will ensure domestic tranquility."[17] Today, no one perceives curbing one's passions or moderating one's opinions as virtues. Instead, people gain social capital and power by letting their passions run amuck, blasting their opinions without concern for others.

When children have no knowledge of how the founding documents or the role religious faith played in America's founding, which the surveys I cited earlier in the book have shown, provided the framework for how a civil society is to operate and thus curb their passion, they grow into adults who have no ability to moderate their behavior or opinions to create a well-ordered society.

In 2020, we witnessed horrific riots in our major cities, often led by Leftist mobs, which resulted in the toppling of statues, burning of buildings, and numerous attacks on our nation's first responders. We have also seen attacks on government buildings by anti-government zealots, such as what happened in Oklahoma City in the mid-1990s by Timothy McVeigh.

Because zealots on both sides lack a working knowledge of our history or system of government, they make up their own rules, which they try to impose by force on everyone else. Neither side has learned healthy societies permit discourse and disagreement about fundamental questions. They are convinced there is only one right side of a story, and they dismiss any other side as illegitimate and unworthy of consideration. A lack of education leads to a lack of tolerance for opposing views; a lack of tolerance leads to violence.

In addition, present generations are growing up with an education that only allows for one side of the debate. The root of this education flows from the top down from our universities, which indoctrinate and train those who then implement radical ideologies in our K-12 schools and throughout all other aspects of our society. When you are convinced there is only one "right" side of a story, it becomes easy to dismiss any other side.

This has been happening on campuses for decades, and what happens on campus never stays on campus. Only a few years ago on the campus of the University of Texas-Austin, some students attempted to set up a pro-life display. One particularly belligerent Leftist kept yelling at them to "Go away!" and then told them "they [the students] had no right to exist."[18]

Once someone has decided another has no right to exist, the next step is to make sure he or she does not exist. That is "cancel culture" in its undiluted form. It is the "trickle-down" effect of our laws and culture when they deny the existence of others, such as the right to life for unborn babies and the elderly or one's ability to freely practice one's faith without government interference, which would be removed under the so-called Equality Act.

John Ellis, professor emeritus at the Left-wing University of Santa Cruz (California), writes how the result of this is a more primitive culture, "On one-party campuses, radical-left faculty have established a political orthodoxy that student mobs enforce, and the political culture of the nation is poisoned as those students take home with them their professors' habit of seeing opinions that differ from theirs as an evil not to be tolerated."[19]

Ellis, like Bari Weiss, whom I quoted earlier in this chapter, agrees that our civilization is regressing—resolving disputes by force instead of commonly agreed upon rules. The result is people live in fear of being physically assaulted, their property vandalized, and or their careers destroyed if they do not fall in line with the orthodoxy of the tribe, whether on the far Left or the far Right, just as we saw in Portland, Seattle, and Washington, DC.[20]

Andrew Michta writing in *National Review*,

> The oligarchization of American elites and the parallel pauperization of the citizenry is the real but uniformly suppressed story behind the country's ongoing Balkanization, . . . We are poised to begin to decompose as a nation along geo-ideological lines, reflecting the territorial alignment of exclusive ideologies, or to witness the triumph of the American Left over a progressively disenfranchised citizenry. If the decline is not stopped soon, the final outcome is likely to repeat the experience of other nations that at some point in their history veered in the direction of a group-based social engineering as a pathway to an allegedly more just society.[21]

Unfortunately, as Michta points out, the result of an effort to create a "more just" society often results in the exact opposite, as George Orwell wrote in *Animal Farm*, "All animals are equal, but some animals are more equal than others."[22]

Going back to the 2018 Woodrow Wilson National Fellowship Foundation test I mentioned earlier, the results clearly illustrate the toll the lack of such an education has taken on our nation. The test, based on a sample of the exam taken for U.S. citizenship, found only 19 percent of those under the age of forty-five could pass in comparison to 74 percent of those over sixty-five.[23] In addition, the other studies I have previously cited document similar results when it comes to knowledge of U.S. history. Given the serious erosion in teaching civics and history started in the late 1960s–early 1970s, it is easy to see the correlation to our current cultural discord.

Areas that would bring people of different political and religious beliefs together, such as professional sports, have now been politicized. If you do not bow to the Leftist cultural orthodoxy, you will not be allowed to sit and enjoy a ballgame with your fellow fans in a stadium or watch in peace with friends and family on your TV. Sporting events, TV shows, movies, and even hometown parades must be "woke" or face condemnation.

People now choose where they shop based on politics, rather than in common places or which business offers the best customer service or prices. And even family members are to be condemned if they do not subscribe to the Leftist orthodoxy young people are being fed—as many parents are finding out when their children return from college or have bought into the cultural orthodoxy presented to them as "acceptable" by the media attacking their values and beliefs.

An example of this has been articles about how people are to confront family members over their politics or religious beliefs during events meant to bring people together such as Thanksgiving and Christmas. Instead of putting our differences aside, several commentators have stated individuals should take this time to either shun or confront family members who do not believe like they do.

Around the holidays in 2016 and 2017, *GQ* magazine, *The Huffington Post*, and *The Establishment* ran articles including talking points and specific ways for people to use Thanksgiving and Christmas dinners to confront and humiliate family members who hold different political views.[24]

Joe Berkowitz, writing in *GQ*, suggested those who did not support President Trump should not offer a handshake to their family members, but in his words, "just stare, disgustedly, at their outstretched arms." He goes on to say they should treat their parents, if they supported the president, with disdain. He advocated they refuse to be alone in a room with their mother because Vice President Pence will never meet one-on-one with another woman besides his wife. He finally recommended they should call their parents by mocking nicknames associated with the president.[25]

This is the outcome of rejecting a shared history and setting one tribe against another because of perceived grievances. Sadly, there are parents whose children have told them they will no longer be allowed to see their grandchildren because they disagree with their conservative political views, and there are parents who have disowned their children because they have embraced Leftist views.

Dennis Prager echoes this in an essay he wrote on the dangers of sending children to public schools to receive a history education based more on grievances than facts. He wrote,

> [N]ot only are these children alienated from their parents' values, but they are often also alienated from the parent(s). One thing you learn when you become left-wing is to have contempt for those who hold other beliefs.
>
> Had these parents known how their children would turn out, they would never have sent them to college—or even to the high school they attended. It appears, however, that no matter how many people lose their children's hearts and minds to left-wing indoctrination, and no matter how much

information accumulates about the perversion of education in American schools, parents continue to take risks with their children they would never take in any other sphere.[26]

How this has played out in our educational system over the past fifty years was eloquently addressed by former Attorney General William Barr in a speech on May 20, 2021. He said,

> [U]p until the 1970s, or so, the instruction received in the public school system openly embraced Judeo-Christian beliefs and values, and most certainly was not hostile to, nor fundamentally in conflict with, traditional religious beliefs . . . .
>
> This is when the Left embarked on a relentless campaign of secularization intent on driving every vestige of traditional religion from the public square. Public schools quickly became the central battleground . . . . [I]t was secularization by subtraction.
>
> Yet even as the schools were forcibly secularized, the notion of moral instruction did not simply go away. The rich Judeo-Christian tradition was replaced with trite talk of liberal values—be a good person, be caring.
>
> But there was no underpinning for those values. What passed for morality had no metaphysical foundation. It is hard to teach that someone ought to behave in a certain way unless you express why.
>
> Values in public schools became really nothing more than mere sentimentality, still drawing on the vapor trails of Christianity. They are a vain attempt

to retain familiar sounding ethics and mores, but without God. When you take away religion, you have left a moral vacuum . . . .

Now we are seeing the affirmative indoctrination of children with a secular belief system and worldview that is a substitute for religion and is antithetical to the beliefs and values of traditional God-centered religion . . . .

In many places in the country, the state of our public schools is becoming an absurdity that can scarcely be believed."[27]

Barr went on to add that schools are not only suppressing the free exercise of religion; they are also promoting a new state secular religion—one dividing rather than uniting. He concluded his speech with these words:

One of the main justifications for the common school movement was that they would be institutions to effectuate the melting pot—to promote our common identity, to promote a solidarity based on being an American. But now the schools have taken on the opposite meaning of separating us, of teaching unbridgeable differences, of dividing us into many different identities destined to be antagonistic. It is all the more alarming and bizarre that the new state-sanctioned ideology challenges the very legitimacy of the nation itself—to the point of explicitly attacking its founding documents, principles, and symbols. If the state-operated schools are now waging war on the nation's moral, historical, philosophical, and religious foundations, then they would seem to have forfeited their legitimacy as the proper vehicle to carry out the mission with which the American people have charged them.[28]

When generations are taught a history based on grievances rather than unity, a once united nation splinters into warring factions of Left vs. Right, poor vs. rich, blacks vs. whites, women vs. men. Yes, as I have stated earlier, there have been injustices we must deal with, and are being dealt with, but for lasting, positive change to occur it must be done through civic dialogue with a thorough understanding of our history and the constitutional principles upon which our nation was established.

That was the intent of America's Founding Fathers, not cultural genocide, as they have been accused of by Leftist historians. Those who founded our nation created a system of government that allowed injustices such as slavery and women's rights to eventually be discarded to the trash bin of history, not enable their perpetuity. Unfortunately, because of the loss of civic knowledge and understanding our heritage, we have become a nation divided against itself, instead of one standing indivisible with liberty and justice for all.

# 5

# *The Perils of Constitutional Ignorance*

*The greatest enemy of knowledge is not ignorance;
it is the illusion of knowledge.*[1]

DANIEL BOORSTEIN

*Academic historians are not much interested
in constitutional history these days. Historians who write
on America's constitutional past are a vanishing breed.*[2]

GORDON WOOD

Younger Americans are woefully ignorant of what is in the U.S. Constitution, which is a major cause of our current national discontents as our citizenry increasingly has no idea how our government works.

A survey of one thousand liberal arts colleges by the American Council of Trustees and Alumni found only 18 percent of these colleges require a class in U.S. history or government for graduation. The same report found nearly

10 percent of college students thought Judge Judy was on the Supreme Court. Forty percent did not know Congress had the power to declare war.

The report concludes, "The way forward is clear. A renewal of civic education can reverse America's civic deficit and restore widespread awareness of our history and government. It is time for students, parents, colleges and universities, and lawmakers to confront the crisis in civic education."[3]

Of the one thousand Americans surveyed in the 2018 "State of the First Amendment" survey done by the Freedom Forum, only *one* person surveyed was able to name all five First Amendment rights: freedom of speech, freedom of religion, freedom of the press, freedom of peaceful assembly, and freedom to petition the government. Even worse, 40 percent could not identify a single First Amendment right.[4]

And Americans do not even know their own rights. A study by the American Revolution Center found only one-third of Americans knew the Bill of Rights includes a right to a jury trial.[5] The same report from the American Council of Trustees and Alumni mentioned earlier found 60 percent of college graduates don't know a single step needed to ratify a constitutional amendment, while 50 percent do not know the term length for members of the House of Representatives and U.S. senators. Finally, 40 percent were unaware it is Congress with the sole power to declare war.[6]

Is it any surprise attacks on many of the fundamental freedoms guaranteed in the U.S. Constitution, particularly regarding freedom of speech and freedom of religion, have occurred?

This is because the Constitution is rarely taught in our educational system, and when it is taught, students are told it is an outdated document needing radical revision to fit the goals of the Leftist agenda.

The second view recognizes the only thing standing in the way of "transforming" America into a Leftist utopian vision is the U.S. Constitution. That is why the confirmation battles over the courts, and particularly the Supreme Court, have become so bitter and destructive over the past thirty-plus years, going back to the confirmation hearings for Judge Robert Bork in 1987. One only need read the late Senator Ted Kennedy's scathing remarks about Judge Bork to realize the contempt Leftists have for an originalist interpretation of the Constitution.

Kennedy said, "Robert Bork's America is a land in which women would be forced into back-alley abortions, blacks would sit at segregated lunch counters, rogue police could break down citizens' doors in midnight raids, schoolchildren could not be taught about evolution, writers and artists could be censored at the whim of the Government, and the doors of the Federal courts would be shut on the fingers of millions of citizens."[7]

These spurious charges, as we see now are better leveled at the Left and which were made on conjecture rather than evidence, were the torch that set off the raging fire of judicial confirmations yet to come—where a judge's qualifications were not evaluated; instead they were being held to their perceived political opinions. Yet, as we have seen numerous times, Supreme Court justices who were figuratively tarred and feathered by the Left, have issued opinions displeasing to conservatives, while Leftist judges have sometimes joined conservative majorities, particularly in First Amendment cases.

## "THE CONSTITUTION IN 2020"

Which leads me to "The Constitution in 2020" project, promoted by Leftist legal figures such as Cass Sunstein, Bruce Ackerman, Robert Post, Harold Koh, Larry Kramer, Noah Feldman, Pam Karlan, William Eskridge, Mark Tushnet, Yochai Benkler, and Richard Ford. This project seeks to implement a progressive constitutional interpretation that would result in a document unrecognizable to its authors and ratifiers.

The new "constitution" would accommodate new "rights" such as guaranteed income, government-funded childcare, increased access to abortion and physician-assisted suicide, liberalization of drug abuse laws, and open borders.[8]

Along with this new "constitution," those who want to fundamentally transform America have proposed simply adding new states, which are already Leftist strongholds. An article in the January 2020 edition of the *Harvard Law Review* argued that 127 new states could be created within the District of Columbia alone.[9] Instead of the United States, our nation would become the United Districts, which would result in greater fragmentation and infighting.

Leftists have also proposed "packing" the Supreme Court with justices who will issue opinions they prefer—an effort they have already launched. While there is no historically defined number of justices, to increase the number of justices simply to get the outcome one desires is a fundamental misunderstanding of the constitutional concept of the court as an impartial interpreter of the law.

It is also a way for Leftists to bypass the manner put in place—via the passage of constitutional amendments—to change the Constitution, which requires two-thirds of the states to ratify an amendment. That was put in place to ensure the people had a say in whatever changes are made or not made.

Because that fundamental understanding of our Constitution and how it can be amended has been lost, politicians today treat the Constitution as sort of a legal Santa Claus: it can be made to grant their wishes if they wear it down with pestering. This is the attitude of court-packers, who believe if they can only get the "right people" on the court, they'll be able to push through their preferred projects. The conversation is not about how best to understand the Constitution and apply it in contemporary America but how best to manipulate and distort it to get what they want.

But the Constitution was never intended to create new rights or give permission to radical projects. It was written to hold America's government accountable to reality. It exists to protect rights bestowed upon us by our Creator. There is plenty of discourse to be had about what those rights are and how to apply them properly; as we learn more about individuals and grow as a society, our understanding of how to protect those rights and extend them equally to all deepens and grows.

That is why the founders built in the mechanism for amending the Constitution. But that is not the conversation Leftists wish to have. To many of them, the Constitution becomes nothing more than a piece of paper where words can be added and deleted in accordance with current cultural whims rather than a guiding document pointing us to truth.

Efforts such as "The Constitution in 2020" are not new. The battle over the Constitution began during the so-called progressive era in the early part of the twentieth century, when the idea of a "living Constitution" first came into being. Progressives such as Oliver Wendell Holmes, Louis Brandeis, and Woodrow Wilson, who developed this idea based on Darwinian evolutionary theory, did not believe in the unalienable rights as declared in the Declaration of Independence and the Constitution.

Wilson said, "Living political constitutions must be Darwinian in structure and in practice."[10] He would later add, "Society is a living organism and must obey the laws of life, not of mechanics; it must develop. All that progressives ask or desire is permission—in an era when 'development,' 'evolution,' is the scientific word—to interpret the Constitution according to the Darwinian principle; all they ask is recognition of the fact that a nation is a living thing and not a machine."[11]

Thus, they sought so-called group rights that evolve with time. As the 1776 Report states, in the view of these progressives, "society has the power and obligation not only to define and grant new rights (such as the right to abortion), but also to take old rights away as the country develops."[12] "Old" rights like freedom of religion, self-defense, and free speech.

While some new rights, such as granting all people, regardless of race, gender, and class the right to vote, righted wrongs and expanded freedom, this mindset has often led to limiting freedom. In many cases, when new rights are granted outside of the framework of the original intent of the Constitution, someone else suffers, such as the unborn child or the businessperson who simply wants to operate their livelihood in accordance with their faith.

For example, when a right to abortion was created, the fundamental right to life as guaranteed under the Constitution was discarded. Human life become a commodity to be disposed of when it is "inconvenient."

Freedom of religion for those who hold a sincere belief that every life is made in the image of God and is sacred or believe sex should be reserved for one man and one woman in a marriage relationship are being tossed aside if they get in the way of personal autonomy or "fulfillment."

Earlier I mentioned the quote from *Animal Farm*, George Orwell's scathing satire on socialism, where the pigs (the political leaders of the barnyard) write a new commandment on the barn wall: "All animals are equal, but some animals are more equal than others."[13] When new rights are created for some, many more lose their rights in return—that is exactly the intent of the so-called Equality Act, which I mentioned earlier. The Equality Act redefines sex to include gender identity and every federally funded entity—most notably schools and colleges—to treat males who declare transgender status as if they were females. It would also stamp out religious exemptions by regulating religious nonprofits and even goes so far as to block the Religious Freedom Restoration Act from applying to its provisions.[14]

The lack of constitutional knowledge gets worse as it slips with each passing generation. How are we going to have a functional society when our society has no idea how it is supposed to function?

And even more importantly, how can people make wise decisions about who their leaders should be if they do not know what those leaders should be doing? As the American Revolution Center notes, "[Our] system of government relies on citizens who are united not by a common race, religion, or country of birth, but rather by belief in a set of ideals as expressed in our founding documents."[15]

If our citizens are not truly united about these ideals, our system of government will collapse because there is nothing else holding it together. That is why the founders of our nation were extraordinary to envision a nation made to work this way—one by the people, for the people, and of the people, as it had never been done before. But for such a government to work requires a united populace based on the greater good for all, rather than a divided populace focusing on what is perceived to be best for a select individual or group.

David Fouse made this point when he wrote, "A government by the people, for the people, and of the people is only as wise, as just, and as free as the people themselves. Ignorance and indifference inevitably erode our freedoms and destroy our republic. It is not without cause that our national discourse in recent years has been so histrionic and hateful."[16]

America has become a country divided against itself, and much of that division is tied to our collective ignorance of our history, heritage, and founding documents.

The 1619 Project is an example of how ignorance breeds division and undermines our national unity. The project is founded on false history, which contributes to a narrative of grievance and group conflict and prevents an actual conversation about racial reconciliation. The Founding Fathers put in place the legal and cultural mechanisms that would eventually end slavery; they did not seek to perpetuate it but rather set up the conditions in which it would end itself.

Whether that was a morally justifiable choice is a valid question, and one historians should ask. But what they eventually intended for slavery is not a valid question; their intentions were clear. As George Will wrote in response to the 1619 Project, "The Constitution was written in 1787 for a nation conscious of its youth. It would grow under a federal government whose constituting document did not acknowledge 'property in man,' and instead acknowledged slaves as persons. This gave slavery no national validation. It left slavery solely a creature of state laws and therefore susceptible to the process that in fact occurred—the process of being regionally confined and put on a path to ultimate extinction. Secession was the South's desperate response when it recognized this impending outcome that the Constitution had facilitated."[17]

If Americans had a true understanding of the Constitution, learned about the context of times when it was written, and had a complete history of what ultimately resulted from it, a free society where all would have equality of opportunity, then such travesties as the 1619 Project would never see the light of day, let alone receive a Pulitzer Prize.

## Striking the Proper Balance

We could have a serious conversation about the justness of the Founders' decision to allow slavery to continue even though they knew it was evil—a question with a great deal of contemporary application. This is the struggle at the core of all political projects: how to balance practical necessity and political ideals. We face this quandary, as we seek to redress injustice in our current moment. We could learn much from the past, if only we allowed the past to teach us instead of obscuring and muddying that past with false narratives.

Progressivism obscures the past on more than just this issue of slavery. Young Americans are increasingly ignorant about America's role in combating communism in the latter half of the twentieth century. More and more young Americans believe the Cold War was purely an economic struggle in which the United States wanted to maintain its position as a world power for its own good. They do not know the Soviet bloc was at the center of a worldwide human rights crisis including genocides, gulags, forced mass starvations, and horrors we have only begun to grasp. Why? Because of the revisionist teaching they have received from Howard Zinn and his like-minded peers.

Young Americans have no sense of the scale of communism's atrocities. The group Victims of Communism reports, a third of millennials are convinced George W. Bush killed more people than Josef Stalin. Nearly half of the older members of Generation Z, born in 1997 and after, say they would vote for a Socialist, with one in five saying they would vote for a Communist.[18] They have absolutely no idea what that means.

Our lack of constitutional knowledge and the abandonment of the Judeo-Christian principles undergirding the Constitution have also led to a profound misunderstanding of the role government plays in the economy. This is another consequence of raising generations of children with either no or grossly distorted historical knowledge.

Yes, as I stated earlier, capitalism is not perfect, and many young people have valid reasons to be disillusioned by the influence massive corporations have in our nation and world. But it is still the best avenue, despite its man-made flaws, for people to independently improve themselves, instead of being made to be dependent with no avenues to pursue other than the government. But when they are learning more about Karl Marx than Adam Smith, their sympathies swing more toward Marx than Smith.

This includes our current leaders, as the leadership of a country only reflects those who put them in power; and much of our leadership are now coming out of the institutions that have either neglected to teach about history and the Constitution or, if they do, present only the distorted views of Howard Zinn and others.

For example, Congresswoman Alexandria Ocasio-Cortez recently said, after a few Supreme Court decisions that did not go the way she wanted, the role of the Supreme Court should be to rubber-stamp the laws Congress passes, rather than interpret them as being constitutional or not.[19]

So, how do we reverse this constitutional ignorance?

Thankfully, there are several organizations such as the Heritage Foundation that offer excellent resources for not only adults to become educated about the U.S. Constitution, but they will be able to then impart that information to the next generation.

While these are excellent resources, the issue still comes back to where most of our nation's children will receive their civic education: in the public, charter, or private school classrooms. Because parents have a greater financial stake in private and charter schools (and private education cannot exist without paying students), they tend to have a greater say in the curriculum being taught, particularly in faith-based schools. There are also private universities such as Hillsdale College in Michigan (which accepts no federal funding with the associated strings attached) teaching solid historical truth and constitutional government. (By the way, Hillsdale offers many free online courses for solid historical, civic, biblical education to everyone. Go to https://online.hillsdale.edu/ to get started.)

This brings us to the public schools, which is a more difficult proposition. Because the public schools in so many municipalities have been captured by those who seek to teach a Leftist view of American history and government, it will take years, and perhaps decades, of perseverance to reverse the damage done and restore the teaching of history and civics as they should be taught. That is why equipping our children at home in this knowledge is so important, as they are likely to be the ones who will someday bring about this restoration.

It is also why those parents who have little or no choice, whether it be for financial or health reasons, but to place their children in public schools must be extra vigilant and expect to receive the full wrath of Leftist activists if they stand up and demand that civics be taught while also standing against the indoctrination their children are receiving. That is the topic of my next chapter.

# 6

# *United We Stand*

*Our civilization is at stake. If we recover our history and the traits that have allowed us to succeed so spectacularly in the past, we will rise to the challenges of the twenty-first century as we have in centuries before. If we fail and the country accepts the narrative that America was rotten to the core from the beginning, we will be lost even if we overcome our external foes and rivals.*[1]

JARRETT STEPMAN

*To present the young people with a full and honest account of our nation's history is to invest them with the spirit of freedom . . . . Depriving the young of the spirit of freedom will deprive us all of our country. It could deprive us, finally, of our humanity itself. This cannot be allowed to continue. It must be stopped.*[2]

LARRY ARNN

*Keeping the spirit of liberty alive in an age of creeping illiberalism is nothing less than our moral obligation. Everything depends on it.*[3]

BARI WEISS

*These principles aren't complicated: work hard, learn from your mistakes, take personal responsibility for your actions. When I made the decisions to get my high school equivalency, attend a community college, and then earn four additional college and university degrees, I believed that my education would open doors. And it did. It was only when exposed to academic theories of oppression in graduate school that I was informed that because I was black, poor, and female, I could never do what I had already accomplished. Thank God, it was too late for these toxic messages to stop me. Don't let them stop you.*[4]

CAROL SWAIN

*History tells us that our schools can be used for both noble and nefarious ends. Stalin knew this. Mao knew this. Castro knew this. Hitler knew this. After all, he's the one who reportedly said, "Let me control the textbooks, and I will control the state." At the end of the day, education is about propagating ideas (good or bad) in the minds, hearts and souls of the generations that follow us.*[5]

EVERETT PIPER

～～

Throughout this book, we have seen the ramifications for our society lacking historical or civic knowledge or an emphasis on *wrong* knowledge about our past. Riots, tribal "warfare," disunity, and the destruction of the American economic system are all symptoms of this problem.

In a recent piece by Benjamin Myers in *The American Conservative*, he spelled out what is at stake if we do not restore the teaching of true American history as well as civics in our nation's schools, colleges, and universities. Myers writes, "There is a battle in the Western world over the continuation of Western civilization, a battle between those who would remember because they understand that memory sustains civilization and those who would forget for the very same reason. One side offers continuity based on a rich cultural inheritance. The other side offers capitulation into darkness and barbarism."[6]

Myers believes we have arrived at a time when our nation's colleges and universities, in particular our Christian colleges and universities, must decide between continuity or barbarism, between light and darkness. That decision will decide the fate of our entire society, as those who leave college and university campuses enter the world.

Myers writes,

> If the liberal arts college doesn't do the work of remembering, then who will? We may continue to have a strong slate of research universities, public and private, dedicated to the next generation of new knowledge, but who will preserve what has already been known for centuries and millennia? . . .
>
> The chant of Jesse Jackson at Stanford—"Hey hey, ho ho, Western Civ has got to go"—has only grown over the past thirty-three years from a commentary on curricula to what is nearly a statement of a negative metaphysics. It is a death wish for a civilization, and it is a widely shared sentiment. The forces of amnesia will not be satisfied until all traces of the past have been eliminated.[7]

Myers believes upholding historical and cultural oblivion requires great courage and conviction. I would add one other thing: perseverance.

The Left's takeover of our nation's institutions did not occur overnight. It has been a steady march going back to the early days of the so-called progressive movement at the beginning of the twentieth century. This includes the revisionist teaching of history, the dumbing down of civic knowledge, and the loss of critical thinking skills among a great deal of our population.

For example, a joint committee of the Illinois state legislature voted in February 2021 to accept a state board of education recommendation that all public school teachers "embrace and encourage progressive viewpoints and perspectives." George Will wrote, "If the board's policy is ratified, Illinois will become a place congenial only to parents who are comfortable consigning their children to 'education' that is political indoctrination, audaciously announced, and comprehensively enforced."[8]

Instead of learning basic life skills such as reading, writing, history, and arithmetic, students are being taught mandated subjects such as black history, women's history, LGBT history, anti-bias and anti-bullying, disability history, and social and emotional learning, to name just a few. Will concludes, "Literature, science, writing, arithmetic? Presumably, if there is any spare time."[9]

## EQUIPPING STUDENTS TO FAIL

Evidently there is not much spare time: In 2019, only 37 percent of third graders in the state could show grade-level proficiency in English language arts and only 41 percent in mathematics.[10] Several other states show equally abysmal results.

For example, on the Left, the Center for American Progress states that while more and more jobs are requiring at least a bachelor's degree, only about one-third of American workers have one. They add that many students who have a high school diploma are not prepared for higher education, as 20 percent of first-year college students must take some sort of remedial course. They conclude, "In other words, a large percentage of students land a high school diploma that is basically meaningless. The document might indicate that the students are ready for college, but in reality, the students simply do not have the necessary skills or knowledge."[11]

The failures of America's educational system have led to the loss of our nation's competitive advantage.[12] For example, literacy rates in American inner-city schools are appalling. A 2015 report by the National Center on Education Statistics found 93 percent of eighth graders are not proficient in reading.[13]

According to the 2015 Program for International Student Assessment, which tests fifteen-year-olds around the world, the math skills of American students have remained stagnant for nearly two decades, falling behind Japan, Poland, and Ireland. U.S. test scores are below the global average. The United States is twenty-fourth out of seventy-one countries in science and thirty-eighth in math. As a result, the U.S. slipped to third in the 2016–17 Global Competitiveness Report, behind Switzerland and Sweden.[14]

The result is a society graduating students with no ability to get and maintain a job, manage their finances, or basically be a functioning human being. Instead, they are being taught to demand perceived injustices be addressed—injustices ironically exacerbated by the horrific education they are receiving that does not provide them with the ability to perform more than a minimum wage job.

Jeff Minick, who has taught history and literature for more than twenty years, wrote in the *Epoch Times*:

> Hear the word "education," and most of us conjure up images of classrooms filled with students bent over their math books, learning grammar and spelling, exploring the parts of a cell, reading about the Battle of Yorktown, or puzzling over "Hamlet."
>
> By the time they graduate high school, we expect these same young people to possess some competence in mathematics and science. After 13 years of schooling, they should know something about our nation's history and the stories of the men and women who helped create our country. They should be familiar on some level with the best of our literature and be able to write clean, well-organized prose devoid of confusion, misspellings, and errors in grammar.
>
> These are the basics of education that produce successful adults and good citizens. Lacking these tools, many young people find themselves facing disadvantages in life, not just when seeking employment but crippled as well by their inability to think critically and to understand the world around them, everything from our Bill of Rights to the causes of inflation.[15]

Eli Steele, a Black, Jewish, and deaf filmmaker discovered this while working on a documentary on young Americans living on the streets. He asked a struggling young man in Chicago about the education he received and how he felt about students being taught to be activists.

The young man replied, "Anyone can march but not everyone can get a job." The man then asked Steele for a job. Steele wrote, "The fact that he was willing to humble himself and ask a perfect stranger for work speaks to the current desperation in his life and it also speaks to his innate knowledge that he knows he needs a job to survive in this country of ours. That's the truth that these new education standards are in danger of betraying."[16]

But that does not deter those who feel the deconstruction of Western civilization trumps receiving a decent education. A high school teacher boasted on social media she was "very proud we got [Homer's] *Odyssey* removed from the curriculum this year!"[17]

But it doesn't stop at Homer. William Shakespeare has also come under assault for his "unwokeness" regarding race, sexuality, gender, and class. A teachers group called #Disrupt Texts said, "This is about white supremacy and colonization."[18] The teachers believe if Shakespeare is taught it can only be done by focusing on equality issues. For example, one instructor decided to add a discussion on "toxic masculinity analysis" to go along with her students reading *Romeo and Juliet*.[19] Another essay added, "A growing number of educators are . . . coming to the conclusion that it's time for Shakespeare to be set aside or deemphasized to make room for modern, diverse, and inclusive voices."[20]

Glynn Custred, a retired anthropology teacher in the California State University system, commented, "The rationale for purging Shakespeare from the curriculum, as formulated in the standard rhetoric of the Left, reveals their agenda, which is the conversion of schools and universities from educational institutions to organs of indoctrination. Since Shakespeare's work has been considered exemplary and universal, these claims must be discredited. Shakespeare's removal from the curriculum and the collective memory is thus mandatory."[21]

Now, granted, knowing Homer and Shakespeare is not a question that will be brought up in a job interview (unless you are applying to teach classics), but it is the critical thinking from reading Homer and Shakespeare that helps adults navigate life. When you remove the concepts learned from Homer and Shakespeare and replace them with nothing, an important part of a child's education is lost.

Earlier in this book, I shared the story of Frederick Douglass. Douglass read the classics, such as Plato, Cato, and Cicero. So did Rev. Dr. Martin Luther King Jr., who cited the teachings of Socrates three times in his famous 1963 "Letter from a Birmingham Jail." These classics gave them both the philosophical arguments and motivation to challenge unjust laws and racial discrimination.

But just in 2021, Howard University, one of America's leading Black universities, announced it was getting rid of its classics department. Howard is eliminating the study of the very classics that inspired Douglass and King.

Cornell West, the professor of practice of public philosophy at Howard University, bemoaned this decision. In a piece cowritten with Jeremy Tate, the founder and CEO of the Classic Learning Trust, West writes,

> Academia's continual campaign to disregard or
> neglect the classics is a sign of spiritual decay, moral
> decline, and deep intellectual narrowness running
> amok in American culture. Those who commit this

terrible act treat Western civilization as either irrel-
evant or not worthy of prioritization or as harmful
and worthy only of condemnation . . . .

The Western canon is, more than anything, a conversation among great thinkers over generations that
grows richer the more we add our own voices and the
excellence of voices from Africa, Asia, Latin America,
and everywhere else in the world. We should never
cancel voices in this conversation, whether that voice
is Homer or students at Howard University. . . . The
removal of the classics is a sign that we, as a culture,
have embraced from the youngest age utilitarian
schooling at the expense of soul-forming education.
To end this spiritual catastrophe, we must restore true
education, mobilizing all of the intellectual and moral
resources we can to create human beings of courage,
vision and civic virtue.[22]

In the competition to be "woke," those cancelling the
classics at Howard University have removed a vital part of the
educational process for Black students. And in July 2021, they
announced they were extending tenure to Nikole Hannah-
Jones, the author of the 1619 Project.[23]

Anika Prather, an adjunct classics professor at Howard,
says classical history is also Black history. She states, "The
world of the ancient times was a really integrated, diverse
society . . . . If we lose it, we lose a piece of all of us. . . . To get
rid of classics or the study of the canon is to disconnect this
current generation from any connection to understanding the
theories that undergird activism as we know it today."[24]

Removing Shakespeare and the classics from curricula is
just the next step after removing the true story of America's

founders. It is all part of the effort to erase culture and create a new culture in line with the Leftist vision. And unfortunately, the Leftists who presently hold power in our nation's higher education system are entrenched and protected with tenure (including Nikole Hannah-Jones).

## SO, WHAT CAN PARENTS DO?

So how do we, as parents, counter this?

It is our responsibility, as West and Tate said, to be training up our children at the earliest age in a classical education that affirms Western civilization, provides critical thinking skills, and provides the tools needed to be constructive and informed citizens.

Many parents have realized this, and it is why they have invested in a classical education for their children—whether it be through private or charter schools. The Left is aware of this movement and seeks to torpedo these schools. Hardly a day goes by without some attack in the media on classical charter schools, or homeschoolers, who are seeking to instill a proper education, free from indoctrination, in their children.

Thankfully, parents in areas like Loudoun County, Virginia, California, Florida, and other areas have awakened to what is being taught to schoolchildren and are taking a stand, only to be ridiculed by the intellectual elite and the media who will spare no expense to advance their Leftist agendas. Both the National Education Association and American Federation of Teachers have announced they will spend millions to take legal action against these parents and their valiant efforts to protect and properly educate their children.[25] This is blatant disregard for the fundamental right of parents to raise their children, and many parents are beginning to realize the educational establishment is not interested in educating, only in indoctrinating.

In addition, some lawmakers are willing to take a stand. Current Florida Governor Ron DeSantis sees the danger of the critical race theory, as embodied by the 1619 Project, and the teachings of Howard Zinn, as a Trojan Horse to undermine Western civilization. When asked if his state would adopt such a school curriculum, he said, "Florida's civics curriculum will incorporate foundational concepts with the best materials, and it will expressly exclude unsanctioned narratives like critical race theory and other unsubstantiated theories. . . . There is no room in our classrooms for things like critical race theory. Teaching kids to hate their country and to hate each other is not worth one red cent of taxpayer money."[26]

Several other governors are not allowing the 1619 Project and critical race theory to be implemented, but that does not mean its advocates will give up. As we have seen many times before, those who seek to radically transform America will never give up and only see losses as temporary setbacks in their efforts to bring an end to the great American experience of ordered liberty.

Earlier in this book, I mentioned what occurred at the Thomas Jefferson High School for Science and Technology. When parents found themselves stonewalled by the administration, they filed a Freedom of Information Act request and received two-hundred-plus pages of internal school emails. These emails exposed the truth: the school's activist principal along with two assistant principals, the director of student services, at least three teachers, several counselors, and a Fairfax County Public Schools "equity" officer deceived parents about all the content for the new critical race theory lesson, masking it as "socio-emotional learning."[27]

Asra Nomani, one of the parents involved, warns parents that it takes vigilance and perseverance to protect their children's learning: "The stealth lesson underscores several serious issues vexing schools today and the future of America. It reveals how school officials circumvent parents as they move aggressively to indoctrinate students in K-12 schools from neighboring Loudoun County, Va., to California. It also serves as a cautionary tale on how important it is that parents assert three rights most districts promise to secure: the right to inspect curriculum . . . the right to opt-out students from certain teachings, including on topics 'sensitive in nature;' and *the right* to have 'controversial issues' discussed 'impartially and objectively.'"[28]

Taking a stand will not be easy. As I have mentioned, the Left is willing to spend countless millions of dollars to indoctrinate schoolchildren while shutting out parents. It may mean personal sacrifice such as placing our children in a classical school, a strong faith-based college, or homeschooling. But for the future of our children, and our country, we must do it. The very future of Western civilization is at stake. But it is encouraging to see so many parents do so, and perhaps this will be the pivotal moment when the teaching of American history is reclaimed from those who seek to use it as an ideological weapon rather than an educational tool.

I say ideological weapon because the far Left is not shy about their hatred of Western civilization, which includes much of the American founding story and the efforts to defend and protect our God-given freedoms. Writing in *National Review*, Andrew Roberts shares a quote from Sonalee Rashatwar, a self-proclaimed Leftist "fat-positivity activist and Instagram therapist," who told the *Philadelphia*

*Inquirer*, "I would love to talk about undoing Western civilization because it's just so romantic to me."[29]

That is the motivation behind such travesties as the 1619 Project, the writings of Howard Zinn, and others who I have discussed in this book. When the truth about our past, regardless whether it is good or bad, is denied, and new "memories" are created, our society loses the foundation upon which it is built. As Stanley Kurtz has noted, the teaching and perpetuation of Western civilization roots people in the past and their values.[30] Without that knowledge and those values, there is no longer anything to bind a society.

Andrew Roberts adds, "The generations who grew up knowing that truth, rather than welting in guilt and self-doubt about 'false consciousness' and so on, were the lucky ones, because they were allowed to study the glories of Western civilization in a way that was unembarrassed, unashamed, and not saddled with accusations of guilt in a centuries-old crime that had absolutely nothing to do with them. They could also learn about the best of their civilization, and how it benefited—and continues to benefit mankind."[31]

Roberts's words are instructive. Regardless what has happened in the past, we should be celebrating what our history and Western civilization has wrought: a society based on the Judeo-Christian principle that all individuals are created in the image of God and worthy of dignity and respect.

Previous generations knew and embraced this. Unfortunately, because they have either been taught no history or only the revisionist history of Howard Zinn, our generation does not. And our country is paying the price.

It is not a coincidence our current cultural condition, and the turn to hard-Left progressivism, started in the late 1950s and into the 1960s, as the teaching of civics and America's true history started to erode and lose influence in American society. Those on the far Left were actively launching attacks—sometimes stealthily—through seizing all the major corridors of cultural and political influence. When these pillars—both key components of the Judeo-Christian principles upon which our nation was founded—started to come under attack, all other principles such as fiscal restraint, freedom of conscience, and limited government came under assault as well.

One of my friends has a saying, "You can't be responsible for what you don't know." Our schoolchildren are deliberately kept in the dark about our history and system of government. They simply do not know better. So, it is difficult to blame them when they act out of ignorance. The destructive behavior of our young people is just a symptom of a greater problem.

That is why it is essential for parents, grandparents, and responsible adults to make sure they learn the truth. Whether we engage our children at an early age in the true story of our nation's history and heritage or make sure their schools teach the complete and accurate picture of our nation's founding or tirelessly refute the misinformation our children may receive, the responsibility is ours. For too long, parents have put their children in the hands of those who will not only withhold the education children need to become functional citizens but actively seek to convert them to a radical agenda.

The trips Craig's parents took him on to see the California missions inoculated him against the rewritten history that would soon be taught in northern California schools. Walking the Freedom Tour in Boston as a family and sharing about the sacrifices made by those who gave their lives to establish a new nation is another activity that can instill true knowledge in children's hearts. Visiting places such as Independence Hall in Philadelphia, Mt. Rushmore, presidential libraries, and the homes of presidents such as Washington, Jefferson, Lincoln, and Eisenhower, to name a few, provides an appreciation for history developed outside the classroom. They also provide learning experiences, as some of these places have sadly been captured by Leftist ideologies, so it allows us, as those who know the true history, to make the necessary corrections to younger generations.

I had a similar experience growing up, one I revisited with my children. First as a child and later as a father, I spent many days at American Revolutionary War sites, Civil War battlefields, and in famous historical museums such as the Smithsonian and the Metropolitan Museum of Art to embed, in my life and in the lives of my sons, the American story.

Patriotism is a delicate balance. It requires that we know and love our nation's story, but it also prohibits us from a blind adoration of our country. As Archbishop Charles Chaput has put it, "zealotry for one's country can be a vice."[32] Those who are overzealous can show profound disrespect for the rule of law, often doing more damage than good by elevating love of country over love of God, family, and their neighbor.

But if we are indifferent to our past, we allow those who seek to destroy our heritage and history free reign to do so. As Archbishop Chaput writes, "But there's also a vice called indifference. And today, in America, we suffer from a media-driven culture that feeds this indifference while simultaneously aggravating divisions. A distorted emphasis on diversity and multiculturalism at the expense of communion and unity discourages any particular loyalty to the nations that constitute the West."[33]

As parents and citizens, we cannot be indifferent, and we cannot allow our children to be indifferent either. We must equip them to be committed citizens with a balanced perspective.

Pushing for more civics and history is not enough. If schools continue to teach the *wrong* civics and history, the problem will just get worse. Rather, we must push schools to teach the right civics and history: courses grounded in balanced historical fact and moral analysis designed to teach students how to respond charitably and ethically to difficult questions of our own time.

Arthur Herman, senior fellow at the Hoover Institute, cautions,

> The real solution isn't boring and bloodless civics courses, which all too often provide cover for the left to sneak in their agenda under the guise of promoting "good citizenship," but teaching American history: the real American history, full of drama, pageantry, struggle, and heartbreak, but also triumph and greatness; and all built around the theme of the constant striving to secure and protect the freedom of the individual.
>
> It's the pursuit of liberty that has united Americans from the beginning and remains our most precious legacy to the future—and defines the epic of American exceptionalism. . . .
>
> From start to finish, however, the epic story would center on how individuals, rich and poor, great, and small, from every race and sex and creed, have discovered and used their freedom in America to advance the freedom of others: as politicians, thinkers and activists, religious and business leaders, and above all as immigrants to a land and country

that gave them the freedom they yearned for and could not find anywhere else. . . .

It's the story of a nation dedicated from its start to a single powerful proposition, that all human beings are endowed by their Creator with certain inalienable rights, and the institutions that govern our society—including our three branches of government and our federal system—were built to secure and protect those rights, and still do today.[34]

Right now, there are two federal bills, under the guise of teaching civics, designed to indoctrinate children instead. The "Civics Learning Act 2021" would provide for $30 million in grant funds for grassroots activism involving "innovative and evidence-based" civics learning and teaching programs.[35] According to Stanley Kurtz of the Ethics and Public Policy Center, these programs include "hands-on civic engagement activities (lobbying and protesting), online and video game-based learning, service learning (in partnership with radical activist organizations), and participation in student governance."[36] These lessons are aimed at elementary school students and are designed to create Leftist activists at the earliest and most impressionable ages.

John Sailer of the National Association of Scholars says this bill is nothing more than an attempt to turn students into professional protestors. Instead of teaching classical history and critical thinking skills, the bill funds so-called action civics. One example is encouraging students to identify an issue, research it, and then pick a "political action item." Students are told this can include writing letters to public officials, petitions, hashtag campaigns, poster campaigns, group awareness activities, and other forms of protest.[37]

While on the surface this might sound well and good—training young people on how to engage in the community on key issues—as Sailer points out, it has nothing to do with civics.

First of all, it does not address the problem that these children still have no idea how our government works and how to engage in civil discourse. Civics education is about teaching students to form their political beliefs, not dictating those beliefs to them (which is presently what is happening through Leftist indoctrination such as critical race theory).

Secondly, Sailer shows how it quickly goes off the rails in the hands of the activist Leftists in the education system. He points to a Rhode Island teacher who strongly suggested students testify against a critical race theory ban and used extra credit as a carrot to dangle to convince them to do so. In addition, groups such as Generation Citizen are providing a list of "approved projects," all of which advance Leftist causes.

Sailer concludes, "For many students learning in such an environment, it would be hard to escape the conclusion that being a good citizen means being a progressive activist."[38]

The second bill, the "Civics Secures Democracy Act"[39] according to Kurtz, promotes critical race theory into all course syllabi. That is how critical race theory suddenly becomes part of physics. It is a radically progressive national civics curriculum, complete with state standards by which schools will be judged. In addition, the National Assessment of Educational Progress (NAEP), which provides annual score cards for America's students, has proposed to help establish the standards and tie all student assessments to those standards. Students and schools will be given little or no say in curricula. Instead, they will be forced to get on board with the new community organizing goals of their civics classes.

So where do we go from here? I believe the authors of the 1776 Project put it best when they say,

> The choice before us now is clear. Will we choose the truths of the Declaration? Or will we fall prey to the false theories that have led too many nations to tyranny? It is our mission—all of us—to restore our national unity by rekindling a brave and honest love for our country and by raising new generations of citizens who not only know the self-evident truths of our founding, but act worthy of them.
>
> This great project of national renewal depends upon true education—not merely training in particular skills, but the formation of citizens. To remain a free people, we must have the knowledge, strength, and virtue of a free people. From families and schools to popular culture and public policy, we must teach our founding principles and the character necessary to live out those principles.
>
> This includes restoring patriotic education that teaches the truth about America. That doesn't mean ignoring the faults in our past, but rather viewing history clearly and wholly, with reverence and love. We must also prioritize personal responsibility and fulfilling the duties we have toward one another as citizens. Above all, we must stand up to the petty tyrants in every sphere who demand that we speak only of America's sins while denying her greatness. At home, in school, at the workplace, and in the world, it is the people—and only the people—who have the power to stand up for America and defend our way of life.[40]

Parents across America must follow the example of the parents at Thomas Jefferson High School for Science and Technology. But there are groups and organizations working to do more.

The National Association of Scholars (NAS) recently launched the Civics Alliance to promote genuine civics education in schools. According to the NAS, the Civics Alliance will

> unite education reformers, policymakers, and every citizen of the United States who wants to preserve civics education that teaches the founding principles and documents of the United States, the key events of American history, the structure of our self-governing federal republic, the functions of government at all levels, how our governing institutions work, and the spirit of liberty and tolerance that should animate our private interactions with our fellow citizens. Such civics education should teach students to take pride in what they share as Americans—an exceptional heritage of freedom, a republic that has succeeded in making liberty a fundamental principle of our government, and the joyful accomplishments of their common national culture.[41]

Another effort is "Free to Learn."[42] This group advocates for education without politics, whether from the Left or the Right. Their mission is to enable children to be free to ask questions, develop individual thoughts and opinions, think critically of ideas and concepts, and be free to achieve. This group will be running advertisements throughout the country to advocate for such an educational approach.

The battle to overcome this darkness is daunting, but by shedding light we can overcome that darkness. As our Founding Fathers wrote, only a moral, righteous, and virtuous people can be free. If future generations are going to enjoy the freedoms we have cherished, we must return to the moral framework that made these freedoms possible in the first place. Once our moral foundation is rebuilt, America's house can once again stand strong.

The battle we are facing is not only a battle for the soul of our nation, but ultimately for the souls of our children, grandchildren, and all generations still to come. The magnitude of the battle we are facing was put best in President Ronald Reagan's 1989 farewell address to the nation. He said,

> An informed patriotism is what we want. And are we doing a good enough job teaching our children what America is and what she represents in the long history of the world? Those of us who are over 35 or so years of age grew up in a different America. We were taught, very directly, what it means to be an American. And we absorbed, almost in the air, a love of country and an appreciation of its institutions. If you didn't get those things from your family, you got them from your neighborhood, from the father down the street who fought in Korea or the family who lost someone at Anzio. Or else you could get a sense of patriotism at school . . . .
>
> [B]ut now, we're about to enter the nineties, and some things have changed. Younger parents aren't sure that an unambivalent appreciation of America is the right thing to teach modern children . . . . We've got to do a better job of getting across that America

is freedom—freedom of speech, freedom of religion, freedom of enterprise. And freedom is special and rare. It's fragile; it needs protection.

So, we've got to teach history based not on what's in fashion but what's important—why the Pilgrims came here, who Jimmy Doolittle was, and what those 30 seconds over Tokyo meant. You know, four years ago, on the 40th anniversary of D-Day, I read a letter from a young woman writing to her late father, who'd fought on Omaha Beach. Her name was Lisa Zanatta Hehn, and she said, "we will always remember, we will never forget, what the boys at Normandy did." Well, let's help her keep her word. If we forget what we did, we won't know who we are. I'm warning of an eradication of the American memory that could result, ultimately, in an erosion of the American spirit. Let's start with some basics: more attention to American history and civic ritual.

And let me offer lesson number one about America: All great change in America begins at the dinner table. So, tomorrow night in the kitchen I hope the talking begins.[43]

The words of our fortieth president could not be more prophetic and more urgent. America is where she is in 2022 because we have either forgotten our past or have rewritten its history to depict our nation as an inhumane disaster instead of a shining city on a hill. If we are to preserve our freedom, if we are to live civilly with each other, and if we are to truly be the United States, instead of the divided states, we must teach future generations our true history and heritage, as well as provide them with the education they need to be capable, responsible citizens.

That is what I want every young American to know again—America is an exceptional nation founded on religious liberty, personal responsibility, and respect for our fellow citizens. It is not a country founded on oppression, hatred for others, and self-interest. No other nation has a system of government based on upholding the dignity of the human individual. If we lose that concept, we will lose our nation and all the freedoms we have come to cherish.

But to maintain that concept, we must rededicate ourselves to the teaching of history—true, verifiable, factual history, with all its glories and tragedies. We need not fear to teach the ugly truths about America alongside the beautiful ones because America's founding vision is pure and her ideals are noble. Our failures do not change that.

Every young American needs to learn the story of a nation with a glorious vision of unity, freedom, and dignity for all. Our story is not straightforward. It is not all good. But at least so far, it is not a tragedy. And if we can restore a common love of our nation—the kind of love that seeks to make her into her best self—it need not become one.

# *Notes*

## INTRODUCTION

1. Ronald Reagan, Farewell Address to the Nation, January 1989.
2. Howard L. Muncy, "Subjects Matter: It Is Past Time to Rescue the Study of History from Its Present Decline," *The Public Discourse*, March 5, 2020, accessed December 21, 2020, https://www.thepublicdiscourse.com/2020/05/60933/.
3. Stanley Kurtz, "Beware: New Civics Mandates Will Be Woke," *National Review*, December 28, 2020, accessed December 28, 2020, https://nationalreview.com/corner/beware-new-civics-mandates-will-be-woke/.
4. https://www.classicalhistorian.com
5. Barbara Danza, "Teaching Children History: Q&A With John De Gree, Founder of The Classical Historian," *The Epoch Times*, April 20, 2021, https://www.theepochtimes.com/teaching-children-history-qa-with-john-de-gree-founder-of-the-classical-historian_3777493.html.
6. Lauren Camera, "U.S. Students Show No Improvement in Math, Reading, Science on International Exam," *U.S. News and World Report*, December 3, 2019, accessed July 6, 2021, https://www.usnews.com/news/education-news/articles/2019-12-03/us-students-show-no-improvement-in-math-reading-science-on-international-exam.
7. William A. Galston, "Why the Young Back Bernie Sanders," *The Wall Street Journal*, February 18, 2020, accessed July 14, 2020, https://www.wsj.com/articles/why-the-young-back-bernie-sanders-11582071616.
8. Algis Valiunas, "Our History Then and Now," *National Affairs*, Winter 2021, accessed January 19, 2021, https://nationalaffairs.com/publications/detail/our-history-then-and-now.
9. Andrew A. Michta, "The American Cultural Revolution Will Leave Scars," *National Review*, February 17, 2021, accessed February 23, 2021, https://www.nationalreview.com/2021/02/the-american-cultural-revolution-will-leave-scars/.

10. Spencer Brown, "Youth Patriotism Index Shows High School Students More Patriotic Than College Peers," *Young America's Foundation*, July 1, 2020, accessed July 2, 2020, https://www.yaf.org/news/youth-patriotism-index-shows-high-school-students-more-patriotic-than-college-peers/.

11. Ben Shapiro, "Stop Surrendering Education to the Radical Left," *The Daily Signal*, July 7, 2021, accessed July 7, 2021, https://www.dailysignal.com/2021/07/07/stop-surrendering-education-to-the-radical-left/.

12. Jeremy Adams, "The Death of Gratitude in the American Classroom," *The Public Discourse*, June 27, 2021, accessed July 6, 2021, https://www.thepublicdiscourse.com/2021/06/76559/.

## CHAPTER 1

1. Letter from James Madison to Thomas Jefferson, October 24, 1787, quoted in Jerry Newcombe, "America's Historical Ignorance," *The Christian Post*, February 21, 2019, accessed May 20, 2020, https://www.christianpost.com/voices/americas-historical-ignorance.html.

2. Dr. Peter Lillback, *Wall of Misconception* (King of Prussia, PA: Providence Forum Press, 2012).

3. Joseph Loconte, "For the Love of Country, Pull Back from the Brink," *National Review*, March 2, 2021, accessed March 4, 2021, https://www.nationalreview.com/2021/03/for-the-love-of-country-pull-back-from-the-brink/.

4. Thomas H. Lee, "What's Keeping David McCullough from Sleeping," *The Wall Street Journal*, March 25, 2018, accessed May 20, 2020, https://www.wsj.com/articles/whats-keeping-david-mccullough-from-sleeping-1522005326.

5. Lee, "What's Keeping David McCullough from Sleeping."

6. "75 Percent of Oklahoma High School Students Can't Name the First President of the U.S.," *News9.com*, September 16, 2009, accessed May 20, 2020, https://www.news9.com/story/5e350348e0c96e774b36 c1c8/75-percent-of-oklahoma-high-school-students-cant-name-the-first-president-of-the-us.

7. "Our Fading Heritage: Americans Fail a Basic Test on Their History and Institutions," Intercollegiate Studies Institute, American Civic Liberty Program, November 20, 2008, 6, 12.

8. "Our Fading Heritage," 12.

9. "Our Fading Heritage," 3.

10. "The American Revolution: Who Cares?" American Revolution Center, December 2, 2009, accessed May 20, 2020, https://www.copy

rightfreecontent.com/human-interest/the-american-revolution-who-cares/.

11. "The American Revolution: Who Cares?"

12. Jarrett Stepman, "Americans Have Almost Entirely Forgotten Their History," *The Daily Signal*, October 4, 2018, accessed May 20, 2020, https://www.dailysignal.com/2018/10/04/american-have-almost-entirely-forgotten-their-history/.

13. Stepman, "Americans Have Almost Entirely Forgotten Their History."

14. David Fouse, "A Republic, If You Can Keep It: The Education Every Student *Really* Needs," *National Review*, March 21, 2017, accessed May 20, 2020, https://www.nationalreview.com/2017/03/americans-history-civics-knowledge-education-federal-government/.

15. Fouse, "A Republic, If You Can Keep It."

16. Max Hastings, "American Universities Declare War on Military History," *Bloomberg.org*, January 31, 2021, accessed February 1, 2021, https://www.bloomberg.com/opinion/articles/2021-01-31/max-hastings-u-s-universities-declare-war-on-military-history.

17. Tami Davis Biddle and Robert M. Citino, "The Role of Military History in the Contemporary Academy," Society for Military History, September 27, 2018, https://www.nationalww2museum.org/war/articles/role-military-history-contemporary-academy.

18. Biddle and Citino, "The Role of Military History in the Contemporary Academy."

19. Laura S. Hamilton, Julia H. Kaufman, and Lynn Hu, "Social Studies Teachers' Perspectives on Key Civic Outcomes in 2010 and 2019: Civic Development in the Era of Truth Decay," RAND Corporation, 2020, accessed February 24, 2021, https://www.rand.org/pubs/research_reports/RRA112-4.html.

20. Laura S. Hamilton, Julia H. Kaufman, and Lynn Hu, "Preparing Children and Youth for Civic Life in the Era of Truth Decay: Insights from the American Teacher Panel," RAND Corporation, 2020, accessed February 24, 2021, https://www.rand.org/pubs/research_reports/RRA1 12-6.html.

21. Newcombe, "America's Historical Ignorance."

22. "Our Fading Heritage," 3.

23. "Our Fading Heritage," 19.

24. Jonah Goldberg, "The Dangers of Arrogant Ignorance," *National Review*, July 7, 2017, https://www.nationalreview.com/2017/07/historical-literacy-lacking-america-ignorance-political-polarization/.

25. George Santayana, *The Life of Reason* (New York: Charles Scribner and Sons, 1905), 284, https://santayana.iupui.edu/wp-content/uploads/2019/01/Common-Sense-ebook.pdf.

26. Stepman, "Americans Have Almost Entirely Forgotten Their History."

27. Stepman, "Americans Have Almost Entirely Forgotten Their History."

28. Fouse, "A Republic, If You Can Keep It."

29. Fouse, "A Republic, If You Can Keep It."

30. Dwight D. Eisenhower, "Inaugural Address: January 20, 1953," *The American Presidency Project*, accessed June 17, 2020, https://www.presidency.ucsb.edu/documents/inaugural-address-3.

31. Zachary Evans and John Loftus, "The Cancel Counter," *National Review*, June 19, 2020, accessed June 20, 2020, https://www.nationalreview.com/news/the-cancel-counter/.

32. Cited by Joel Achenbach, "U.S. Grant Was the Great Hero of the Civil War but Lost Favor with Historians," The Washington Post, April 24, 2014, https://www.washingtonpost.com/national/health-science/us-grant-was-the-great-hero-of-the-civil-war-but-lost-favor-with-historians/2014/04/24/62f5439e-bf53-11e3-b574-f8748871856a_story.html.

33. Achenbach, "U.S. Grant."

34. Achenbach, "U.S. Grant."

35. Evans and Loftus, "The Cancel Counter."

36. Evans and Loftus, "The Cancel Counter."

37. Ganesh Setty and Leah Asmelash, "The Theodore Roosevelt statue in front of New York's Museum of Natural History will finally be removed," CNN, June 24, 2021, accessed July 6, 2021, https://www.cnn.com/2021/06/24/us/theodore-roosevelt-statue-new-york-trnd/index.html.

38. Amanda Prestgiacomo, "Watch: Activist Who Supports Statue Removal Reveals On-Air She Doesn't Know Who Winston Churchill Is," *The Daily Wire*, June 15, 2020, accessed June 16, 2020, https://www.dailywire.com/news/watch-activist-who-supports-statue-removal-reveals-live-on-air-she-doesnt-know-who-winstonchurchill-is.

39. Prestgiacomo, "Watch."

40. Sean Kane, "Myths & Misunderstandings: Grant as a Slaveholder," *American Civil War Museum*, November 21, 2017, accessed July 6, 2021, https://acwm.org/blog/myths-misunderstandings-grant-slaveholder/.

41. Christopher F. Rufo, "Critical Race Theory: What It Is and How to Fight It," *Imprimis* 50:3, March 2021, accessed July 8, 2021, https://imprimis.hillsdale.edu/critical-race-theory-fight/.

42. Rufo, "Critical Race Theory."
43. Rufo, "Critical Race Theory."
44. Abraham Lincoln, House Divided Speech, June 16, 1858, accessed June 23, 2020, https://www.abrahamlincolnonline.com/lincoln/speeches/house.htm.
45. Rufo, "Critical Race Theory."
46. Rufo, "Critical Race Theory."

## CHAPTER 2

1. Joshua Pauling, "No Teacher Neutrality," *Salvo Magazine,* Spring 2021, 12, accessed March 22, 2021, https://salvomag.com/article/salvo 56/no-teacher-neutrality.
2. G. K. Chesterton, *Illustrated London News,* May 13, 1911.
3. Kathryn Jean Lopez, "Dismantling of a Culture," interview with David Gelernter, *National Review,* July 18, 2012, accessed December 28, 2020, https://www.nationalreview.com/2012/07/dismantling-culture-interview/.
4. Amor Towles, *A Gentleman in Moscow: A Novel* (New York: Penguin Books, 2019), 144.
5. Wilfred M. McClay, *Land of Hope: An Invitation to the Great American Story* (New York: Encounter Books, 2019). xiv.
6. "Attorney General William P. Barr Delivers Remarks to the Law School and the de Nicola Center for Ethics and Culture at the University of Notre Dame," the United States Department of Justice, October 11, 2019, accessed February 1, 2020, https://www.justice.gov/opa/speech/attorney-general-william-p-barr-delivers-remarks-law-school-and-de-nicola-center-ethics.
7. Franklin Roosevelt, "The Four Freedoms," State of the Union Address, January 6, 1941, accessed July 6, 2021, https://voicesofdemocracy.umd.edu/fdr-the-four-freedoms-speech-text/.
8. Roosevelt, "The Four Freedoms."
9. Roosevelt, "The Four Freedoms."
10. "From John Adams to Massachusetts Militia, 11 October 1798," *Founders Online,* National Archives, accessed January 4, 2021, https://founders.archives.gov/documents/Adams/99-02-02-3102.
11. Salvatore Joseph Cordileone, "Statues of Saint Junipero Serra Deserve to Stay," *Washington Post,* June 30, 2020, accessed July 6, 2020, https://www.washingtonpost.com/opinions/2020/06/30/statues-saint-junipero-serra-deserves-stay/.
12. "Statue of Junipero Serra Toppled in Downtown Sacramento Protest," CBS13 Sacramento, July 5, 2020, accessed July 6, 2020, https://

sacramento.cbslocal.com/2020/07/05/statue-of-junipero-serra-toppled-in-downtown-sacramento-protest/.

13. George Orwell, *1984* (London: Secker & Warburg, 1949).

14. Natalie Swaby, "UW Black Student Union pushes for removal of George Washington statue," King5.com, February 15, 2021, accessed February 23, 2021, https://www.king5.com/article/news/community/facing-race/uws-bsu-pushing-for-changes-on-campus-including-removal-of-the-george-washington-statue/281-69444f15-8d36-4a73-9a42-beb6d5603ec7.

15. Anne Snyder and Leon Kass, "Forging a People, Sustaining a Nation," May 14, 2021, accessed July 6, 2021, https://breakingground.us/forging-a-people-sustaining-a-nation/.

16. Jarrett Stepman, *The War on History: The Conspiracy to Rewrite America's Past* (Washington, DC: Regnery, 2019), xiii.

17. Stepman, *The War on History*.

18. Lauren Lumpkin, "George Washington University to Consider Shedding Controversial Colonials Moniker," *The Washington Post*, July 22, 2020, accessed August 3, 2020, https://www.washingtonpost.com/local/education/george-washington-university-to-consider-shedding-controversial-colonials-moniker/2020/07/22/d27c5300-cb78-11ea-91f1-28aca4d833a0_story.html.

19. Ryan Gaydos, "George Washington University Drops Colonials Moniker, Officials Say Name Fails to 'Match the Values of GW,'" *Fox News*, June 15, 2022, accessed June 17, 2022, https://www.foxnews.com/sports/george-washington-university-drops-colonials.

20. Lumpkin, "George Washington University to Consider Shedding Controversial Colonels Moniker."

21. Joshua Q. Nelson, "University of Washington Student Union Pushes to Remove George Washington Statue on Campus," *Fox News*, February 23, 2021, accessed July 6, 2021, https://www.foxnews.com/us/university-washington-students-remove-george-washington-statue.

22. "Chicago Mayor Lori Lightfoot considers tearing down 41 monuments across the city, including statues of Lincoln and Washington," *KNewz.com*, February 19, 2021, accessed February 23, 2021, https://knewz.com/chicago-monuments-under-review/.

23. Grant Addison, "Frisco's Folly," *Washington Examiner*, February 11, 2021, accessed February 23, 2021, https://www.washingtonexaminer.com/politics/friscos-folly.

24. Jocelyn Gecker and Haven Daley, "San Francisco to strip Washington, Lincoln from school names," Associated Press, January 27, 2021, https://abcnews.go.com/Politics/wireStory/san-francisco-strip-washington-lincoln-school-names-75519114.

25. Stella Chan and Amanda Jackson, "San Francisco Unified School District Board pauses its plan to rename 44 of its schools to focus on reopening," *CNN.com*, February 22, 2021, accessed February 23, 2021, https://www.cnn.com/2021/02/22/us/san-francisco-school-name-changes-paused-trnd/index.html.

26. "California's Ethnic Studies Mandate," *Wall Street Journal*, March 16, 2021, accessed March 18, 2021, https://www.wsj.com/articles/californias-ethnic-studies-mandate-11615935133.

27. "California's Ethnic Studies Mandate."

28. Sam Dorman, "California Proposes Curriculum with Chanting Name of Aztec God Who Accepts Human Sacrifice," *Fox News*, March 11, 2021, accessed March 18, 2021, https://www.foxnews.com/us/california-schools-aztec-gods.

29. "Against California's Ethnic-Studies Curriculum," *National Review*, March 18, 2021, accessed March 18, 2021 https://www.nationalreview.com/2021/03/against-californias-ethnic-studies-curriculum.

30. Bret Stephens, "California's Ethnic Studies Follies," *New York Times*, March 9, 2021, accessed March 18, 2021, https://www.nytimes.com/2021/03/09/opinion/californias-ethnic-studies.html.

31. Stephens, "California's Ethnic Studies Follies."

32. https://www.britannica.com/topic/slavery-sociology/Historical-survey

33. "Washington's Changing Views on Slavery," accessed July 6, 2021, https://www.mountvernon.org/george-washington/slavery/washingtons-changing-views-on-slavery/.

34. Glenn C. Loury, "The Case for Black Patriotism," *City Journal*, Spring 2021, accessed April 20, 2021, https://www.city-journal.org/the-case-for-black-patriotism.

35. Kay C. James, "Mal-Educated Rioters and Spineless Politicians Wage a War Against Democracy," *The Washington Times*, July 13, 2020, accessed August 3, 2020, https://www.washingtontimes.com/news/2020/jul/13/mal-educated-rioters-and-spineless-politicians-wag/.

36. Quoted in Wilfred McCray, "Of Statues and Symbolic Murder," *First Things*, June 26, 2020, accessed August 3, 2020, https://www.firstthings.com/web-exclusives/2020/06/of-statues-and-symbolic-murder.

37. McCray, "Of Statues and Symbolic Murder."

38. McCray, "Of Statues and Symbolic Murder," 77.

39. Kyle Smith, "Al Sharpton Puts Jefferson Memorial on Notice," *National Review*, August 16, 2017, accessed December 29, 2020, http://www.nationalreview.com/corner/450537/al-sharpton-opposes-jefferson-memorial.

40. Stepman, *The War on History*, 79.

41. McCray, "Of Statues and Symbolic Murder."

42. Martin Luther King Jr., "'I Have a Dream,' August 28, 1963," The Avalon Project, accessed December 29, 2020, http://avalon.law.yale.edu/20th_century/mlk01.asp.

43. Carol Swain, "What I Can Teach You About Racism," PragerU, April 4, 2021, accessed April 5, 2021, https://ugetube.com/watch/what-i-can-teach-you-about-racism-mp4_PSeL6fZlPu8tsp5.html.

44. James P. Byrd, *A Holy Baptism of Fire and Blood: The Bible and the American Civil War* (Oxford, UK: Oxford University Press, 2021).

45. Kate Hardiman, "Most College Students Think America Invented Slavery, Professor Finds," *The College Fix*, October 31, 2016, accessed December 29, 2020, https://www.thecollegefix.com/college-students-think-america-invented-slavery-professor-finds/

46. Quoted in Bernard Mayo, *Jefferson Himself: The Personal Narrative of a Many-sided American* (Charlottesville, VA: University Press of Virginia, 1998), 109.

47. Stepman, *The War on History*, 86.

48. "Respected Historical Figures Who Were Actually Terrible People," *Grunge.com*, accessed July 6, 2021, updated December 7, 2021, https://www.grunge.com/69542/respected-historical-figures-actually-terrible-people/.

49. Bari Weiss, "The Self-Silencing Majority," *Deseret News*, March 2, 2021, accessed March 10, 2021, https://www.deseret.com/indepth/2021/3/2/22309605/the-silenced-majority-bari-weiss-new-york-times-cancel-culture-free-speech-democrat-republican.

50. Weiss, "The Self-Silencing Majority."

51. Melissa Korn, "UCLA Faces Probe Over Review of Lecturer Who Used N-Word in Class," *Wall Street Journal*, June 25, 2020, accessed July 6, 2021, https://www.wsj.com/articles/ucla-faces-probe-over-review-of-lecturer-who-used-n-word-in-class-11593114216.

52. Weiss, "The Self-Silencing Majority."

53. Andrew A. Michta, "The Captive Mind and America's Resegregation," *Wall Street Journal*, July 31, 2020, accessed August 3, 2020, https://www.wsj.com/articles/the-captive-mind-and-americas-resegregation-11596222112.

54. Frederick Douglass, "Oration in Memory of Abraham Lincoln," April 14, 1876, Teaching American History, accessed June 28, 2020, https://teachingamericanhistory.org/library/document/oration-in-memory-of-abraham-lincoln/.

55. See "Frederick Douglass Statue," Architect of the Capitol, https://www.aoc.gov/explore-capitol-campus/art/frederick-douglass-statue.

56. Thomas Catenacci, "Vandals Tear Down Statue of Frederick Douglass, Drag It to River," the Daily Signal, July 6, 2020, accessed July 6, 2021, https://www.dailysignal.com/2020/07/06/statue-of-black-abolitionist-frederick-douglass-torn-down-dragged-to-nearby-river/.

57. Nikole Hannah-Jones, "The 1619 Project," *The New York Times,* August 14, 2019, https://www.nytimes.com/interactive/2019/08/14/magazine/black-history-american-democracy.html.

58. Hannah-Jones, "The 1619 Project."

59. Twitter comment cited in Tyler O'Neil, "1619 Project Founder Admits It's 'Not About History,' But a Fight to 'Control the National Narrative,'" July 29, 2020, accessed September 23, 2020, www.pjmedia.com/culture/tyler-o-neil/2020/7/20/1619-founder-admits-its-not-a-history-but-a-fight-to-control-the-national-narrative-n724944.

60. "The 1619 Project," *The New York Times,* August 14, 2019, accessed July 1, 2020, https://www.nytimes.com/interactive/2019/08/14/magazine/1619-america-slavery.html.

61. Nikole Hannah-Jones, "America Was Not a Democracy Until Black Americans Made it One," *New York Times,* August 14, 2019, accessed July 8, 2021, https://www.nytimes.com/interactive/2019/08/14/magazine/black-history-american-democracy.html.

62. Leslie M. Harris, "I Helped Fact-Check the 1619 Project. The Times Ignored Me," *Politico.com,* March 6, 2020, accessed July 6. 2020, https://www.politico.com/news/magazine/2020/03/06/1619-project-new-york-times-mistake-122248.

63. Harris, "I Helped Fact-Check the 1619 Project. The Times Ignored Me."

64. Michael Guasco, "The Misguided Focus on 1619 as the Beginning of Slavery in the U.S. Damages Our Understanding of American History," *Smithsonian* magazine, September 13, 2017, accessed February 1, 2021, https://www.smithsonianmag.com/history/misguided-focus-1619-beginning-slavery-us-damages-our-understanding-american-history-180964873/.

65. Becket Adams, "1619 Project Founder Claims Her Project is Simply an 'Origin Story,' Not History," *Washington Examiner,* July 28, 2020, accessed July 7, 2021, https://www.washingtonexaminer.com/opinion/1619-project-founder-claims-her-project-is-simply-an-origin-story-not-history.

66. Stephen L. Miller @redsteeze, Twitter, July 28, 2020, https://twitter.com/redsteeze/status/1287987731721646082/photo/2.

67. Sara E. Wilson, "Arthur M. Schlesinger, Jr. National Humanities Medal, 1998," *National Endowment for the Humanities,* accessed January 19,

2021, https://www.neh.gov/about/awards/national-humanities-medals/arthur-m-schlesinger-jr.

68. O'Neil, "1619 Project Founder Admits It's 'Not About History.'"

69. "The Spirit of 1776," *National Review,* January 22, 2021, accessed January 22, 2021, https://www.nationalreview.com/2021/01/the-spirit-of-1776/.

70. Hannah Farrow, "The 1619 Curriculum Taught in Over 4,500 Schools – Frederick County Has the Option," *Medill News Service,* July 21, 2020, https://dc.medill.northwestern.edu/blog/2020/07/21/the-1619-curriculum-being-taught-in-over-4500-schools-frederick-county-has-the-option/.

71. Erwin Lutzer, *We Will Not Be Silenced* (Eugene, OR: Harvest House Publishers, 2020), 51.

72. Tyler O'Neil, "Andy Ngo's Testimony Implicates 'Peaceful Protestors' in Antifa Violence," August 4, 2020, accessed June 16, 2022, https://pjmedia.com/news-and-politics/tyler-o-neil/2020/08/04/andy-ngo-antifa-and-its-allies-have-made-rioting-an-art-form-in-portland-n752106.

73. O'Neil, "Andy Ngo's Testimony Implicates 'Peaceful Protestors' in Antifa Violence."

74. Andrew Ujifusa, "Biden Administration Cites 1619 Project as Inspiration in History Grant Proposal," updated May 3, 2021, https://www.edweek.org/teaching-learning/biden-administration-cites-1619-project-as-inspiration-in-history-grant-proposal/2021/04.

75. Dennis Prager, "Most American Schools Are Damaging Your Child," March 9, 2021, accessed March 18, 2021, https://dennisprager.com/column/most-american-schools-are-damaging-your-child/.

76. "The 1776 Report," the President's Advisory 1776 Commission, January 2021, 1.

77. David Harsanyi, "The Ridiculous Attacks on the 1776 Report," *National Review,* January 19, 2021, accessed January 21, 2021, https://www.nationalreview.com/corner/the-ridiculous-attacks-on-the-1776-report/.

78. Harsanyi, "The Ridiculous Attacks on the 1776 Report."

79. Harsanyi, "The Ridiculous Attacks on the 1776 Report."

80. Victor Davis Hanson, "Thoughts on the 1776 Commission and Its Report," *National Review,* January 21, 2021, accessed January 21, 2021, https://www.nationalreview.com/2021/01/thoughts-on-the-1776-commission-and-its-report/#slide-1/.

81. "The 1776 Report," the President's Advisory 1776 Commission, January 2021, 1–2.

82. Ibid, 11.

83. Ibid.

84. "The Spirit of 1776."

85. Hanson, "Thoughts on the 1776 Commission and Its Report."

86. Hanson, "Thoughts on the 1776 Commission and Its Report."

87. Lindsey Burke, PhD, Jonathan Butcher, Emilie Kao, and Mike Gonzalez, "The Culture of American K–12 Education: A National Survey of Parents and School Board Members," The Heritage Foundation, January 11, 2021, accessed February 24, 2021, https://www.heritage.org/education/report/the-culture-american-k-12-education-national-survey-parents-and-school-board.

88. "The Spirit of 1776."

89. "The Spirit of 1776."

90. James Varney, "Biden Administration Offers Grants to Teach Children '1619 Project,' Inherent Racism Central to U.S.," *Washington Times*, April 21, 2021, accessed April 22, 2021, https://www.washingtontimes.com/news/2021/apr/21/biden-administration-offers-grants-teach-children-/.

91. Jarrett Stepman, "The Woke Managerial Revolution Goes to School," *The Daily Signal,* December 10, 2020, accessed December 21, 2020, https://www.dailysignal.com/2020/12/10/the-woke-managerial-revolution-goes-to-school/.

92. Caslee Sims, "Virginia School District Cancels Dr. Seuss Celebration, Citing 'Racial Undertones' In His Books," *CBS17.com,* March 1, 2021, accessed March 2, 2021, https://www.cbs17.com/news/south/virginia-school-district-cancels-dr-seuss-celebration-citing-racial-undertones-in-his-books/.

93. "California's Radical Indoctrination," *The Wall Street Journal,* August 30, 2020, accessed December 21, 2020, https://www.wsj.com/articles/californias-radical-indoctrination-11598829048.

94. Asra Q. Nomani, "IndoctriNation: No. 1 U.S. High School Pushes Racist Activism On Students," *The Federalist,* April 20, 2021, accessed April 22, 2021, https://thefederalist.com/2021/04/20/indoctrination-no-1-u-s-high-school-pushes-racist-activism-on-students/.

95. Lutzer, *We Will Not Be Silenced,* 43.

96. Chesterton, *Illustrated London News.*

97. Joseph Pearce, "Chesterton and the Meaning of Education," *The Imaginative Conservative,* January 26, 2021, accessed March 4, 2021, https://theimaginativeconservative.org/2021/01/chesterton-meaning-education-joseph-pearce.html.

98. "Meeting of the 1776 Commission," May 24, 2021, https://www.hillsdale.edu/news-and-media/press-releases/meeting-of-the-1776-commission/.

99. "Meeting of the 1776 Commission."

## CHAPTER 3

1. "Howard Zinn on Civil Disobedience," 2007 interview reprinted in 2018, accessed March 24, 2021, https://www.howardzinn.org/state-of-nature-zinn-civil-disobedience/.

2. Howard Zinn, *Vietnam: The Logic of Withdrawal* (Boston: Beacon Press, 1967), 89, 101; cited in Mary Grabar, *Debunking Howard Zinn: Exposing the Fake History That Turned a Generation Against America* (Washington, DC: Regnery, 2019), 210.

3. Robin West, *Progressive Constitutionalism: Reconstructing the Fourteenth Amendment* (Durham, NC: Duke University Press, 1994), 17–18.

4. Mary Kay Linge, "Public Schools Are Teaching Our Children to Hate America," *New York Post,* February 22, 2020, accessed October 20, 2020, https://www.nypost.com/2020/02/22/public-schools-are-teaching-our-children-to-hate-america/.

5. Louis Jacobson, "Is book by Howard Zinn the 'most popular' high-school history textbook?," PolitiFact, April 15, 2015, https://www.politifact.com/factchecks/2015/apr/15/rick-santorum/book-howard-zinn-most-popular-high-school-history-/.

6. Mary Grabar, "Howard Zinn's Anti-American Propaganda Takes Over the Smithsonian," *The Federalist,* August 21, 2019, https://thefederalist.com/2019/08/21/howard-zinns-anti-american-propaganda-takes-smithsonian/.

7. "Making History," *The New York Times,* July 1, 2007, accessed July 6, 2021, https://www.nytimes.com/2007/07/01/books/review/Letters-t-1.html.

8. Krystina Skurk, "Debunking Left-Wing Historian Howard Zinn Is Like Shooting Fish in a Barrel," *The Federalist,* February 8, 2020, accessed October 20, 2020, https://thefederalist.com/2020/02/08/debunking-left-wing-historian-howard-zinn-is-like-shooting-fish-in-a-barrel/.

9. Grabar, *Debunking Howard Zinn,* xi.

10. Dissident Prof: Resisting the Re-education of America, https://dissidentprof.com/about.

11. Grabar, *Debunking Howard Zinn,* 25.

12. Grabar, *Debunking Howard Zinn.*

13. Grabar, *Debunking Howard Zinn,* xiii-xiv.

14. Howard Zinn, *A People's History of the United States* (New York: Harper Collins, 1980).

15. Zinn, *A People's History of the United States,* 73.

16. Zinn, *A People's History of the United States,* 96.

17    Allen Lutins, transcribed; and Jim Tarzia, *The Communist Manifesto* by Karl Marx and Friedrich Engels, accessed July 6, 2021, https://www.fulltextarchive.com/pdfs/The-Communist-Manifesto.pdf.

18. Howard Zinn, *You Can't Be Neutral on a Moving Train* (Boston: Beacon Press, 1994), 175.

19. Grabar, *Debunking Howard Zinn*, 104.

20. Zinn, *A People's History of the United States*, 70.

21. Zinn, *A People's History of the United States*, 417.

22. Zinn, *A People's History of the United States*, 9.

23. Statement on the Standards of Professional Conduct (updated 2019), American Historical Association, accessed July 6, 2021, https://www.historians.org/jobs-and-professional-development/statements-standards-and guidelines-of-the-discipline/statement-on-standards-of-professional-conduct.

24. Grabar, "Howard Zinn's Anti-American Propaganda Takes Over the Smithsonian."

25. Grabar, *Debunking Howard Zinn*, 25.

26. Zinn, *A People's History of the United States*, 8.

27. Graber, *Debunking Howard Zinn*, 25.

28. Grabar, *Debunking Howard Zinn*, 4.

29. Jennifer C. Braceras, "The Intellectual Roots of the War Against Columbus," October 9, 2018, http://jenniferbraceras.com/the-intellectual-roots-of-the-war-against-columbus/.

30. Daniel Webster, "The Plymouth Oration," December 22, 1820, accessed December 29, 2020, https://www.dartmouth.edu/~dwebster/speeches.plymouth-oration.html.

31. Jarrett Stepman, *The War on History: The Conspiracy to Rewrite America's Past* (Washington, DC: Regnery, 2019), 62.

32. Stepman, *The War on History*, 65.

33. Stepman, *The War on History*, 59.

34. Zinn, *A People's History of the United States*, 410.

35. Zinn, *A People's History of the United States*, 407–8.

36. Zinn, *A People's History of the United States*, 469.

37. Mary Grabar, "The Perils of Revisionist History," the Heritage Foundation, August 28, 2020, https://www.heritage.org/civil-society/event/virtual-event-the-perils-revisionist-history.

38. Grabar, *Debunking Howard Zinn*, 3.

39. Skurk, "Debunking Left-Wing Historian Howard Zinn Is Like Shooting Fish in a Barrel."

40. Skurk, "Debunking Left-Wing Historian Howard Zinn Is Like Shooting Fish in a Barrel."

41. David Greenberg, "Agit-Prof: Howard Zinn's influential mutilations of American history," the New Republic, March 18, 2013.

42. Sam Wineburg, "Undue Certainty: Where Howard Zinn's *A People's History* Falls Short," *American Educator,* Winter 2012–13.

43. Grabar, *Debunking Howard Zinn,* xiii.

44. Wineburg, "Undue Certainty."

45. Greenberg, "Agit-Prof."

46. Felix Salmon, "Gen Z Prefers 'Socialism' to 'Capitalism,'" *Axios. com,* January 27, 2019, accessed July 7, 2021, https://www.axios.com/exclusive-poll-young-americans-embracing-socialism-b051907a-87a8-4f61-9e6e-0db75f7edc4a.html.

47. Zachary Mettler, "Declining Number of College Students Describe Themselves as 'Patriotic,'" *The Daily Citizen,* April 30, 2020.

48. Senator Orrin Hatch, "America Is Facing a Civics Crisis: Here's How to Fix It," *Washington Times,* March 29, 2021, accessed April 6, 2021, https://www.washingtontimes.com/news/2021/mar/29/america-is-facing-a-civics-crisis-heres-how-to-fix/.

49. Grabar, *Debunking Howard Zinn,* xi.

50. Zinn, *A People's History of the United States,* 9.

51. Grabar, *Debunking Howard Zinn,* 56, citing Robert Cohen, "Mentor to the Movement: Howard Zinn, SNCC, and the Spelman College Struggle," in *Howard Zinn's Southern Diary,* 17.

52. Beth Feeley is a freelance writer and editor for various nonprofit organizations, including the Woodson Center, serving as launch director for its "1776" effort. Previously, Beth worked in consulting and public relations for Hill and Knowlton and Arthur Andersen for a variety of Fortune 500 companies and most recently served as editor at the Policy Circle. Beth also runs a local civic organization, New Trier Neighbors, which promotes common sense policies in local government and schools.

53. Beth Feeley, "The Schoolwork My Kids Are Bringing Home Exposes Public Schools' Radical Leftist Policies," *The Federalist,* April 6, 2020, accessed December 15, 2020, https://thefederalist.com/2020/04/06/the-schoolwork-my-kids-are-bringing-home-exposes-public-schools-radical-leftist-politics/.

54. Fred Siegel, "History and Politics: A Common Fate," *Academic Questions,* December 1991, 32–36.

55. Grabar, *Debunking Howard Zinn,* 89.

56. Grabar, *Debunking Howard Zinn,* 107.

57. Joy Pullmann, "How To Replace Howard Zinn's Communist Account of U.S. History for American Kids," *The Federalist,* August 28, 2019, accessed December 22, 2020, https://thefederalist.com/2019/08/28/replace-howard-zinns-communist-account-u-s-history-american-kids/.

# CHAPTER 4

1. Alexander Solzhenitsyn, *The Gulag Archipelago* (New York: HarperCollins, 1973).

2. Benjamin Myers, "How Liberal Arts Colleges Could Save Civilization," *The American Conservative,* November 25, 2020, accessed December 21, 2020, https://www.theamericanconservative.com/articles/culture-war-memory-and-the-liberal-arts/.

3. Moses Maimonides, *The Guide for the Perplexed,* ca. 1190.

4. Abraham Lincoln, "House Divided Speech," Springfield, IL, June 16, 1858, accessed April 12, 2021, http://www.abrahamlincolnonline.org/lincoln/speeches/house.htm.

5. Michael Dimock and Richard Wike, "America Is Exceptional in the Nature of Its Political Divide," *Pew Research Center,* November 13, 2020, accessed July 7, 2021, https://www.pewresearch.org/fact-tank/2020/11/13/america-is-exceptional-in-the-nature-of-its-political-divide/.

6. Thomas Carothers and Andrew O'Donohue, "How Americans Were Driven to Extremes," *Foreign Affairs,* September 25, 2019, accessed July 7, 2021, https://www.foreignaffairs.com/articles/united-states/2019-09-25/how-americans-were-driven-extremes.

7. Jennifer Harper, "47% of Americans 'Feel Like a Stranger in Their Own Country,'" *Washington Times,* November 1, 2018, accessed November 11, 2020, https://www.washingtontimes.com/news/2018/nov/1/47-of-americans-feel-like-a-stranger-in-their-own/.

8. Selim Algar, "Largest US Teachers Union Vows to 'Fight Back' Against CRT Critics," *New York Post,* July 4, 2021, accessed July 7, 2021, https://nypost.com/2021/07/04/teachers-union-vows-to-fight-back-against-critical-race-theory-critics/.

9. "The 1776 Report," the President's Advisory 1776 Commission, January 2021, 12.

10. Yuval Levin, *Our Fractured Republic* (New York, Basic Books, 2016), 79.

11. Joseph Loconte and Samuel Gregg, "For the Love of Country, Pull Back from the Brink," *National Review,* March 2, 2021, accessed March 4, 2021, https://www.nationalreview.com/2021/03/for-the-love-of-country-pull-back-from-the-brink/.

12. Bari Weiss, "The Self-Silencing Majority," *Deseret News,* March 2, 2021, accessed March 10, 2021, https://www.deseret.com/indepth/2021/3/2/22309605/the-silenced-majority-bari-weiss-new-york-times-cancel-culture-free-speech-democrat-republican.

13. Weiss, "The Self-Silencing Majority."

14. Weiss, "The Self-Silencing Majority."

15. Victor Davis Hanson, "Are We on the Verge of Civil War?" *National Review,* September 21, 2018, accessed July 7, 2020, https://www.nationalreview.com/2018/09/american-divide-culture-politicization-polarization/.

16. John Roberts, "2019 Year-End Report on the Federal Judiciary," December 2019, https://www.supremecourt.gov/publicinfo/year-end/20 19year-endreport.pdf.

17. Irving Kristol, "Republican Institutions vs. Servile Institutions," speech, May 1974, Poynter Center, Indiana University.

18. Alliance Defending Freedom, video, 2002.

19. John M. Ellis, "Woke Universities Lead America to a Primitive State," *Wall Street Journal,* November 2, 2020, accessed December 21, 2020, https://www.wsj.com/articles/woke-universities-lead-america-to-a-primitive-state-11604359918.

20. Ellis, "Woke Universities Lead America to a Primitive State."

21. Andrew A. Michta, "The Fracturing of the American Ideal," *National Review,* February 7, 2021, accessed February 18, 2021, https://www.nationalreview.com/2021/02/the-fracturing-of-the-american-ideal/.

22. George Orwell, *Animal Farm* (London: Secker and Warburg, 1945).

23. Jarrett Stepman, "Americans Have Almost Entirely Forgotten Their History," *The Daily Signal,* October 4, 2018, accessed May 20, 2020, https://www.dailysignal.com/2018/10/04/american-have-almost-entirely-forgotten-their-history/.

24. Examples include Joe Berkowitz, "It's Your Civic Duty to Ruin Thanksgiving by Bringing Up Trump," *GQ,* November 21, 2017, accessed May 15, 2018, https://www.gq.com/story/the-case-for-ruining-thanksgiving; Peter Van Buren, "How to Talk with Trump-Hating Millennials This Thanksgiving," *The American Conservative,* November 22, 2017, accessed May 15, 2018, http://www.theamericanconservative.com/articles/how-to-talk-to-trump-hating-millennials-this-thankgiving/; Derrick Lemos, "This Thanksgiving, Stand Up to Your Relatives Who Helped Elect Trump, *The Establishment,* November 10, 2016, accessed May 15, 2018, https://theestablishment.co/your-friends-and-relatives-did-this-now-what-can-you-do-695ff8ddc260.

25. Berkowitz, "It's Your Civic Duty to Ruin Thanksgiving by Bringing Up Trump."

26. Dennis Prager, "Most American Schools Are Damaging Your Child," March 9, 2021, accessed March 18, 2021, https://dennisprager.com/column/most-american-schools-are-damaging-your-child/.

27. William Barr, "Edwin Meese III Award for Originalism and Religious Liberty Acceptance Speech," May 20, 2021, accessed July 7, 2021, https://adflegal.org/william-barr-interview.

28. Barr, "Edwin Meese III Award for Originalism and Religious Liberty Acceptance Speech."

## CHAPTER 5

1. Cited in Jonah Goldberg, "The Dangers of Arrogant Ignorance," *National Review*, July 7, 2017, https://www.nationalreview.com/2017/07/historical-literacy-lacking-america-ignorance-political-polarization/.

2. Gordon Wood is Alva O. Way University Professor at Brown University and the 2011 recipient of the National Humanities Medal. Quoted in "A Crisis in Civic Education," American Council of Trustees and Alumni, January 2016, accessed March 4, 2021, https://www.goacta.org/wp-content/uploads/ee/download/A_Crisis_in_Civic_Education.pdf.

3. "A Crisis in Civic Education."

4. Carlin Becker, "Sad! Survey Shows Shocking Percentage of Americans Unable to Name a Single First Amendment Right," *Independent Journal Review*, August 4, 2018, accessed August 6, 2018, https://ijrnew.flywheelsites.com/percentage-americans-first-amendment/.

5. "The American Revolution, Who Cares?," American Revolution Center, December 2, 2009, accessed May 20, 2020, https://www.copyrightfreecontent.com/human-interest/the-american-revolution-who-cares/, 11.

6. David Fouse, "A Republic, If You Can Keep It: The Education Every Student *Really* Needs," *National Review*, March 21, 2017, accessed May 20, 2020, https://www.nationalreview.com/2017/03/americans-history-civics-knowledge-education-federal-government/.

7. "Edward Kennedy Delivers 'Robert Bork's America' Speech, Earning Him the Title of 'Liberal Lion,'" July 1, 1987, accessed July 7, 2021, https://worldhistoryproject.org/1987/7/1/edward-kennedy-delivers-robert-borks-america-speech-earning-him-the-title-of-liberal-lion.

8. Jack M. Balkin and Reva B. Siegel, *The Constitution in 2020* (London: Oxford University Press, 2009).

9. "Pack the Union: A Proposal to Admit New States for the Purpose of Amending the Constitution to Ensure Equal Representation," *Harvard Law Review*, January 10, 2020, accessed January 19, 2020, https://harvardlawreview.org/2020/01/pack-the-union-a-proposal-to-admit-new-states-for-the-purpose-of-amending-the-constitution-to-ensure-equal-representation/.

10    Woodrow Wilson, *Constitutional Government in the United States* (New York: Columbia University Press, 1908), 57.

11. Ronald J. Pestritto, *Woodrow Wilson: The Essential Political Writings* (Lanham, MD: Lexington Press, 2005), 121.

12. "The 1776 Report," the President's Advisory 1776 Commission, January 2021, 13.

13. George Orwell, *Animal Farm* (London: Secker and Warburg, 1945).

14. "Against the Equality Act," *National Review*, February 25, 2021, accessed July 7, 2021, https://www.nationalreview.com/2021/02/against-the-equality-act/.

15. "The American Revolution: Who Cares?"

16. Fouse, "A Republic: If You Can Keep It."

17. George Will, "A Pulitzer Rewarding Slovenliness and Ideological Ax-Grinding," *Manchester Union Leader*, May 8, 2020, accessed May 12, 2020, https://www.unionleader.com/opinion/columnists/george-f-will-a-pulitzer-rewarding-slovenliness-and-ideological-ax-grinding/article_e34683e5-1368-5a.

18. Jeff Minick, "Saving Liberty One Child at a Time," *The Epoch Times*, April 20, 2021, accessed April 21, 2021, https://www.theepochtimes.com/saving-liberty-one-child-at-a-time_3777540.html.

19. Brad Polumbo, "AOC just revealed her dangerous constitutional illiteracy," *Washington Examiner*, April 17, 2021, accessed April 19, 2021, https://www.washingtonexaminer.com/opinion/aoc-just-revealed-her-dangerous-constitutional-illiteracy.

## CHAPTER 6

1. Jarrett Stepman, *The War on History: The Conspiracy to Rewrite America's Past* (Washington, DC: Regnery, 2019), xv.

2. Larry P. Arnn, "Orwell's *1984* and Today," *Imprimis* 49:12, December 2020, accessed March 4, 2021, https://imprimis.hillsdale.edu/orwells-1984-today/.

3. Bari Weiss, "The Self-Silencing Majority, *Deseret News*, March 2, 2021, accessed March 10, 2021, https://www.deseret.com/indepth/2021/3/2/22309605/the-silenced-majority-bari-weiss-new-york-times-cancel-culture-free-speech-democrat-republican.

4. Carol Swain, "What I Can Teach You About Racism," PragerU, April 4, 2021, accessed April 5, 2021, https://ugetube.com/watch/what-i-can-teach-you-about-racism-mp4_PSeL6fZlPu8tsp5.html.

5. Everett Piper, "President Biden, why bother sending our kids back to school?" *Washington Times*, March 28, 2021, accessed April 6,

2021, https://www.washingtontimes.com/news/2021/mar/28/president-biden-why-bother-sending-our-kids-back-t/.

6. Benjamin Myers, "How Liberal Arts Colleges Could Save Civilization," the American Conservative, November 25, 2020, https://www.theamericanconservative.com/articles/culture-war-memory-and-the-liberal-arts/.

7. Myers, "How Liberal Arts Colleges Could Save Civilization."

8. George Will, "In Illinois, Indoctrination Could Replace Education," *Washington Post Writers Group,* February 6, 2021.

9. Will, "In Illinois, Indoctrination Could Replace Education."

10. Will, "In Illinois, Indoctrination Could Replace Education."

11. Ulrich Boser, Perpetual Baffour, and Steph Vela, "A Look at the Education Crisis: Tests, Standards, and the Future of American Education," January 2016, accessed June 27, 2018, https://cdn.americanprogress.org/wp-content/uploads/2016/01/26105959/TUDAreport2.pdf.

12. Kimberly Amadeo, "U.S. Education Rankings Are Falling Behind the Rest of the World," the Balance, updated April 13, 2022, first accessed June 14, 2018, https://www.thebalance.com/the-u-s-is-losing-its-competitive-advantage-3306225.

13. "2015 Reading Trial Urban District Snapshot Report, Detroit, Grade 8, Public Schools," Institute of Education Sciences, National Center for Education Statistics, accessed June 16, 2018, https://nces.ed.gov/nationsreportcard/subject/publications/dst2015/pdf/2016048XR8.pdf.

14. "2015 Reading Trial Urban District Snapshot Report, Detroit, Grade 8, Public Schools."

15. Jeff Minick, "More Than Just the Basics: Educating Our Children for Life," *The Epoch Times,* July 6, 2021, accessed July 7, 2021, https://www.theepochtimes.com/more-than-just-the-basics-educating-our-children-for-life_3882880.html.

16. Eli Steele, "Illiterate Revolutionaries," *Fox News,* February 18, 2021, accessed February 18, 2021, https://www.foxnews.com/us/chicago-schools-illinois-progressive-politics-teaching-standards-inclusive.

17. Michael W. Chapman, "High School Teacher Boasts of Banning Homer's 'The Odyssey' From the Curriculum," *CNSNews.com,* January 4, 2021, accessed March 24, 2021, https://www.cnsnews.com/blog/michael-w-chapman/high-school-teacher-boasts-banning-homers-odyssey-curriculum.

18. James Varney, "Woke Teachers Want Shakespeare Cut from Curriculum: 'This Is about White Supremacy,'" *Washington Times,* February 15, 2021, accessed February 18, 2021, https://www.washingtontimes.com/news/2021/feb/15/woke-teachers-want-shakespeare-cut-curriculum-abou/.

19. Varney, "Woke Teachers Want Shakespeare Cut from Curriculum."

20. Varney, "Woke Teachers Want Shakespeare Cut from Curriculum."

21. Varney, "Woke Teachers Want Shakespeare Cut from Curriculum."

22. Cornel West and Jeremy Tate, "Howard University's removal of classics is a spiritual catastrophe," *Washington Post,* April 19, 2021, accessed April 20, 2021, https://www.washingtonpost.com/opinions/2021/04/19/cornel-west-howard-classics/.

23. Tom Foreman Jr. and Aaron Morrison, "Tenure Struggle Ends with Hannah-Jones Charting New Course," July 6, 2021, accessed July 7, 2021, https://news.yahoo.com/nikole-hannah-jones-she-not-122249992.html.

24. Lauren Lumpkin, "Students and faculty fight to save classics department at Howard University," *Washington Post,* April 20, 2021, accessed April 21, 2021, https://www.washingtonpost.com/education/2021/04/20/howard-university-classics-department-dissolve/.

25. Hannah Natanson, "Amid critical race theory controversy, teachers union chief vows legal action to defend teaching of 'honest history,'" *Washington Post,* July 6, 2021, accessed July 7, 2021, https://www.washingtonpost.com/local/education/teachers-union-critical-race-theory-weingarten/2021/07/06/ef327c20-de61-11eb-9f54-7eee10b5fcd2_story.html; Brittany Bernstein, "Nation's Largest Teachers' Union to Conduct Opposition Research on CRT Opponents," *National Review,* July 2, 2021, accessed July 7, 2021, https://www.nationalreview.com/news/nations-largest-teachers-union-to-conduct-opposition-research-on-crt-opponents/.

26. Rachel del Guidice, "'No Room' for Critical Race Theory in Florida Schools, Gov. Ron DeSantis Says," *The Daily Signal,* March 18, 2021, accessed March 20, 2021, https://www.dailysignal.com/2021/03/18/no-room-for-critical-race-theory-in-florida-schools-gov-ron-desantis-says/.

27. Asra Q. Nomani, "IndoctriNation: No. 1 U.S. High School Pushes Racist Activism On Students," *The Federalist,* April 20, 2021, accessed April 22, 2021, https://thefederalist.com/2021/04/20/indoctrination-no-1-u-s-high-school-pushes-racist-activism-on-students/.

28. Nomani, "IndoctriNation."

29. Andrew Roberts, "Why We Must Teach Western Civilization," *National Review,* May 18, 2020, accessed January 6, 2020, https://www.nationalreview.com/magazine/2020/05/18/why-we-must-teach-western-civilization/.

30. Roberts, "Why We Must Teach Western Civilization."

31. Roberts, "Why We Must Teach Western Civilization."

32. Charles J. Chaput, "*Dulce et Decorum Est*: In Defense of Healthy Patriotism," *The Public Discourse*, March 7, 2021, accessed March 18, 2021, https://www.thepublicdiscourse.com/2021/03/74524/.

33. Chaput, "*Dulce et Decorum Est.*"

34. Arthur Herman, "Message to DeSantis—Civics Important But Here's What We Really Need to Teach Our Kids," *Fox News*, March 21, 2021, accessed March 22, 2021, https://www.foxnews.com/opinion/desantis-message-history-civics-freedom-arthur-herman.

35. H.R.400 - 117th Congress (2021–2022): Civics Learning Act of 2021, Congress.gov

36. Stanley Kurtz, "Dems Want $30 Million for Student Protests," *National Review*, March 8, 2021, accessed July 7, 2021, https://www.nationalreview.com/corner/dems-want-30-million-for-student-protests/.

37. John Sailer, "Training Students to Protest Doesn't a Civics Education Make," *Washington Times*, July 6, 2021, accessed July 8, 2021, https://www.washingtontimes.com/news/2021/jul/6/training-students-to-protest-doesnt-a-civics-educa/.

38. Sailer, "Training Students to Protest Doesn't a Civics Education Make."

39. See https://sites.google.com/icivics.org/supportcivics/summary.

40. "The 1776 Report," the President's Advisory 1776 Commission, January 2021, 16.

41. "The Civics Alliance: A Toolkit" and "Scholars Announce Launch of the Civics Alliance," National Association of Scholars, March 22, 2021, https://www.nas.org/blogs/article/the-civics-alliance-a-toolkit and https://www.nas.org/blogs/press_release/scholars-announce-launch-of-the-civics-alliance.

42. www.freetolearn.org

43. Ronald Reagan, Farewell Address to the Nation, January 11, 1989, Ronald Reagan Presidential Library & Museum, accessed January 12, 2021, https://reaganlibrary.gov/archives/speeches/farewell-address-to-the-nation/.